The Weimar Republic

*A Captivating Guide to the History of
Germany Between the End of World War I
and Rise of the Nazi Era*

Free Bonus from Captivating History
(Available for a Limited time)

Hi History Lovers!

Now you have a chance to join our exclusive history list so you can get your first history ebook for free as well as discounts and a potential to get more history books for free! Simply visit the link below to join.

Captivatinghistory.com/ebook

Also, make sure to follow us on Facebook, Twitter and Youtube by searching for Captivating History.

Contents

Introduction

Although Adolf Hitler is one of the most notorious and well-known characters in modern history, few people know that his rise to iron-fisted dictatorship actually began in the waning days of the democratic Weimar Republic.

Born from the ruins of World War I, this little-known republic could be thought of as less than a geographical place and more of an era for a well-known country—Germany. The Weimar Republic, Germany's first democratic government, was named after its birthplace, the German city of Weimar.

Though only in existence for a brief fourteen years, a virtual blip in history, its story is fascinating and important. With nearly half the men in the country fighting an unwinnable war in 1918, Germany was on the brink of starvation, economic collapse, and mutiny. Those who survived the 1916/17 winter, which they called the "Turnip Winter," a bitter name given from the indignity of having to eat food they saw fit only for cattle, could hardly dream of having meat to eat. Hunger riots rocked the streets of Berlin, and workers went on strike, as they were fed up with unlivable wages and poor working conditions. Inspired by the recent Russian Revolution, talk of revolt permeated the air.

Faced with problems on every front, Germany had some difficult decisions. Disenchanted with the monarchy of Kaiser Wilhelm II and seeking to appease the Allied nations, their answer was the Weimar Republic. Understanding the mutinous events that led up to its existence, how it was instituted to fix a desperate situation within the country, and the reasons it failed gives us insight into how Germany gave rise to one of the most infamous dictators in all of history.

Weimar's history also shows how Allied countries that were reeling from the brutality of World War I and their attempts to console themselves with reparations and a treaty actually helped lay the groundwork for World War II.

Chapter 1 – The Kiel Mutiny

The officers knew it was a suicide mission. In fact, the night before, many of them partied and drank, toasting the "death ride of the German navy." Negotiations for an armistice with the Allies had been underway for the last few weeks, but none of the eighty thousand sailors assigned to be involved with the unsanctioned Operation Plan #19 was seeking the infamy of being sacrificed in an apocalyptic last-ditch sea battle effort.

Imperial Naval Commander Admiral Franz von Hipper had become impatient with the restructuring of the government and efforts at peace being undertaken by Kaiser Wilhelm II. Hoping that a show of movement toward democracy would appease the Allies during the peace negotiations, the Kaiser appointed Prince Maximilian von Baden as the new chancellor at the beginning of October 1918. He was backed by a cabinet of Social Democrats.

Von Hipper knew that his audacious last battle plan would be put down if he presented it to von Baden. So, he decided he wouldn't present it and would just go ahead without permission. Perhaps seeking a last shot at glory or to save the honor of the fleet, von Hipper went ahead with his naval order, giving it twenty days later on October 24th.

War-weary sailors were already long discontented with the conditions imposed upon them on their ships. Their food rations were not only inadequate, but they were also of poor quality and utterly monotonous. To add insult to injury, the sailors watched as officers enjoyed delicious feasts at banquets while they languished in their separated cramped quarters. Officers enjoyed relative comfort aboard the battleships and dreadnaughts. The physical separation from the officers gave the sailors a sense of growing isolation, and it made it seem as if the officers were indifferent to their suffering. It created fertile ground for complaints to be aired among the groups of disgruntled men bunking together.

The constant discussion of grievances caused the men to reach a boiling point, and the talk was sure to eventually give way to action. Many of their fellow soldiers had already deserted, having escaped into German port towns and disguising themselves as citizens. What actions could those still aboard the ships take?

Now the men who had stayed in their assignments were asked to sacrifice again for their final daring mission of the war. The German fleet was planning coordinated attacks against the Allied forces at the mouth of the Thames and in the English Channel near northern France. Of course, the sailors were no cowards; they were willing to fight if attacked first. But to go into battle unprovoked was another story. What would it accomplish if Germany was about to agree to the armistice with the Allies anyway? Did they really want to take part in an action that might derail peace negotiations with the Allied forces? It was no surprise that a mutiny was brewing.

At the end of October 1918, the first mutinous crews finally broke. Germany's fleet was docked just north of the town of Wilhelmshaven, waiting to leave for battle. The rumblings of rebellion began on October 28th, with crews aboard numerous ships defying orders from their commanders. It wasn't long before the situation escalated.

Leading the revolution was a young Kaiserliche Marine, a boiler stoker on the Helgoland named Ernst Wollweber. Men aboard the docked SMS Thüringen and the SMS Helgoland began to sabotage their own ships. They seized many of their officers, locking them in their cabins. They began to sabotage the ships, putting out the fires that ran the boilers and disabling the engines, ensuring that they would not and could not set sail. Navigation lights were smashed, further crippling the ships.

The crews of several other battleships followed suit and joined in the mutiny. Reports from a number of ships in the Third Navy Squadron cried of a multitude of insubordinate acts from their sailors. Crew members belonging to the SMS Derfflinger and SMS Von der Tann flat-out refused to return from shore leave.

Soon, shouts of "down with Kaiser Wilhelm" thundered from the decks of other ships. As the fervor began to spread, Vice Admiral Hugo Kraft took action to halt its spread among his Third Navy Squadron, ordering them away from the docks and into a nearby bight where they would be quarantined from the rebellion. But it was too late. The battleship SMS Markgraf already contained dozens of rebel ringleaders.

However, the mutiny was not a universal action among the fleet. The men on the torpedo boats, who had not suffered the same indignities that those on the larger ships complained of, had not seen fit to rebel. In fact, they turned on their revolutionary fleet mates.

Maneuvering around, they aimed their torpedoes at the ships that instigated the trouble. With their own fleet now against them and poised to strike, the crews of the Thüringen and Helgoland had no choice but to surrender. Kraft, too, was quick to ferret out the rebels from the Markgraf.

The relatively peaceful surrender of those on the Thüringen, Helgoland, Markgraf, and other ships did not let the rebels off the hook. Over one thousand men were arrested for mutiny. These men were rounded up and sent to military prisons in Kiel. But these men who had mutinied were not hardened dissenters; rather, they were loyal navy men who had simply been pushed to their limits. The military action von Hipper had proposed pushed them past those limits. It could have been argued that they were in more need of compassion than punishment given the circumstances. Fellow sailors tried to come to their defense.

Going into the city, sailors chose a delegation to represent them and their demands. That delegation banded with local workers and trade union members in Kiel. The group designated themselves as the Workers' and Soldiers' Council.

On November 1st, 250 men met at the Union House to make their demands. Aside from wanting the release of their fellow soldiers arrested for mutiny, they took the opportunity to demand better conditions on their ships. They also demanded that the "suicide mission" against the British be called off.

The council would not get any satisfactory concessions that night. Police came into the Union House and dispersed the gathering. The action did nothing to deter the council and those who stood with them. In fact, it was quite the opposite. The men were further inflamed, and they began to plan an even larger meeting.

The next day, led by torpedo factory worker Karl Artelt and Kiel Soldiers' Council founder Lothar Popp, thousands gathered at Kiel's military drill grounds to demonstrate. This time, instead of police, government troops were sent in to quash the brewing rebellion. Artelt and Popp confronted the troops, convincing them to allow the protestors to depart peacefully. But the protesters were not done.

At High Seas Fleet High Command, Admiral von Hipper learned of the mutiny. Knowing there was no way to carry out the operation now, he canceled the battle, his last chance at glory and honor lost.

Employing the same strategy of divide and conquer that Vice Admiral Kraft had used to try to separate his squadron from the instigators, von Hipper ordered the squadrons away from Kiel. Only the Third Squadron remained there. But instead of containing the trouble, the tactic had the opposite effect—it helped spread the idea of revolt up and down the coast.

Though the initial reason for the mutiny was now gone, the trouble was just beginning. The battle was canceled too late, the damage had already been done, and the seeds of revolt had already begun to spread.

Chapter 2 – From Protest to Revolution

"We saw the horses collapse on the road, just out of weakness and hunger. How the people rushed to these dead fallen animals and cut out the meat."—Gertrud Volcker

On November 3rd, 1918, several thousand military and civilian workers walked off their job sites and joined together on the drill grounds. Still keeping the original agenda, Artelt called for support in freeing the imprisoned mutineers. But many of those gathered had more immediate concerns and agendas of their own.

Like the sailors, civilians were also tired of the war and the tribulations it brought them and their families. They wanted to see the country returned to order and a relief from the hardships the war had placed on them. Not least of these consequences was hunger. Hundreds of thousands of Berlin factory workers had protested the same issue in 1917. If they had thought the reduced rations of that year were difficult, the hardship had only intensified.

Their desperation for an end to the war and want of food was reflected in the placards the protesters held up calling for "Frieden und Brot." The sailors were equally tired of war and hunger, and they also called for the release of the imprisoned sailors.

That cause finally moved the crowd toward additional actions, but for some, it would be a fatal move. At 7 p.m., a mass of protesters, close to three thousand, marched toward the military prison nearest Waldwiese. Motivated less by organization and more by rising hysteria, the crowd was nearing a frenzy. The sheer numbers of the mob that approached the prison was enough to cause the quick release of the mutinous prisoners inside.

Pleased with their success, the crowd pressed on toward the large naval prison located on the Feldstrasse. Along the way, they disarmed patrols who attempted to stop them. Their numbers swelled as more men poured out of taverns to join with the marching crowd.

As they drew closer to the prison, their progress was suddenly blocked by a patrol of forty-eight troops led by Lieutenant Steinhäuser. Determined not to fall to the crowd as the other patrols had, these men were ready to stand their ground. Immediately, Steinhäuser shouted for the crowd to stop. The mob pressed on. Fearing they would be disarmed by the overwhelmingly larger force, the troops fired their weapons into the air. When the menacing crowd continued to move on them, innocuous warning shots turned into direct fire, with troops shooting right into the midst of the crowd. The protestors were momentarily stunned. Their surprise quickly turned to rage, and they returned the troops' fire with some gunshots of their own, along with a hail of rocks.

Fortunately, before long, the metaphorical cavalry arrived to assist the beleaguered patrol. Trucks full of heavily armed patrols screeched onto the scene, backed by trucks from Kiel's fire department. Quickly realizing that they had become outgunned and outmanned, the crowd dispersed and left.

When the smoke cleared, the bodies of eight men lay in the streets. Among the thirty-nine seriously wounded was Lieutenant Steinhäuser, who sustained a severe head injury after being struck by a stone.

Believing his men had returned order to Kiel, naval station governor Wilhelm Souchon called off his panicked request for additional forces. Going a step further, he had his own troops disarmed and scattered around Kiel. It was a grave misjudgment. Souchon, who was out of touch with his men, seemed to have little idea of the rage that continued to simmer among his sailors. For them, this was far from over. The bloody conflict of November 3rd may have temporarily halted the rebellion, but it moved the men to swear oaths of vengeance. Thousands of embittered sailors vowed to finish the fight that they started with their own navy.

That same night, Souchon was struck by the gravity of his error. In a memo to naval command, he maintained confidence that he had everything under control yet fully expected trouble in the shipyards the next day.

Giving credence to the sailors' grievances that their commanders kept themselves removed from the feelings of their crews, the next day (November 4th), Captain Bartels, commander of the First Torpedo Division, gave a very ill-advised and highly ill-timed speech to his men. Chastising them for the protests, he shouted, "Soldiers are not to meddle in politics! Soldiers will obey, soldiers must obey, and soldiers do obey." If he thought that speech would bring the men to order, he was sorely mistaken.

Incensed, Karl Artelt immediately leaped onto the table and demanded the formation of a soldiers' council. Officers jumped to seize him and try to drag him from the table, but his fellow sailors immediately came to his defense, "mercilessly" raining punches down onto the officers, disarming them.

Fired up, the men made for the armory and procured weapons for themselves. They also hastily put together the council as Artelt had suggested, electing him to be the chairman. From there, the rebellion continued to spread.

Sailors who did not join the rebellion refused to act against their mates, and those who did openly revolt commandeered their ships and threatened any other vessel that made a move against the rebels on shore.

Souchon was stunned. He went from victory the night before to now having lost control of every unit in Kiel. Not a single above-seas unit would obey his orders. Troops that did go out to meet the rebels either turned back or joined the mutineers as they met them.

As the rebellion spread, Souchon knew he had lost. Kiel was now under the control of forty thousand soldiers, sailors, and workers. With little troop support behind him and knowing that all other options would be hopelessly suicidal, he opted for the only reasonable course of action—capitulation and an agreement to hear the men's grievances and demands.

That night, two representatives from the central government arrived to discuss negotiations—Secretary of State Conrad Haussmann and Socialist Party Deputy Gustav Noske. Arriving at the train station, Noske was ready to sweep in and restore order to the town. But when he disembarked, his stern demeanor quickly turned to bewilderment. Instead of seeing riotous mutineers protesting or engaged in violence or other tumultuous behavior, he was greeted by the sailors with wild cheering.

As Noske was driven through the town in a car bearing the symbolic red flag, with his driver hoarsely shouting, "Long live freedom!" over and over again, he noted something else about the people he saw. Rather than an air of revolution, there was an atmosphere of celebration. In the minds of the sailors, the moment Souchon and the representatives agreed to meet with their soldiers' council, they had won. It didn't matter that the demands had yet to be laid out and that the negotiations still had to take place—they celebrated as if it were a done deal. He heard the sounds of joy everywhere—laughter floating up from the streets and soldiers confidently flirting with girls. Had a revolution actually taken place in this town? The only sign that it had was the red flag insignias seen everywhere.

Stopping, Noske decided to give an impromptu speech. Surely, his call for order would sober the mood. Instead, he was met with applause, which further perplexed him. The light mood that he witnessed quickly changed soon enough. Toward the end of his speech, shots rang out. The audience quickly scattered, and Noske demanded to know what was going on.

As he and Hausmann arrived at naval headquarters to meet with the officers and council representatives, the joy, celebration, and lightheartedness of earlier had given way to chaos, confusion, and disorder. As the meeting started, the sailors confidently presented their case—a list of fourteen demands, reminiscent of United States President Woodrow Wilson's Fourteen Points speech. The demands they made were mostly military instead of political—among them calling for the release of imprisoned sailors, better treatment for the enlisted men, and recognition of the council's authority as representatives.

Just when the government representatives may have wondered why they were called to negotiate demands specific to the military, they were likely stunned by the brazen political demands that came next. The council called for the German monarchy and the Prussian House of Lords to be dissolved and a fair representation of the people to be allowed. These demands were clearly above the capacity of Noske and Haussmann to concede to, but it set the stage for what was about to come.

By the next morning, November 5th, Kiel had descended into "revolutionary chaos." Within a few days, Noske was able to get the situation in Kiel under control. But he could not control where the seeds of revolution had already blown. Though a government proclamation was issued condemning the rebellion, it could not contain the growing crisis. As the navy's officer corps internally collapsed, what began as a protest was turning into an all-out rebellion. And it continued its rise among the military and civilians alike.

Chapter 3 – The Collapse of the German Monarchy and the Birth of the "Accidental Republic"

"Tiredness of the war, rejection of the old political powers, yes, but there was no readiness to do something constructively for it. 'This will be done by those on top,' was a common saying also among the organized workers, 'they will do it all right.'"—Julius Bredenbek, member of the Workers' Youth in 1918.

The base commander at Kiel, Crown Prince Heinrich, knew he was in danger. One by one, the Kaiser's flags were lowered from ships as men across the Imperial German Navy fleet replaced them with red flags, their symbol of protest. Only one commander, Karl Wilhelm Weniger, captain of the König, attempted to stop the red flag from being raised on his ship. He and two staff members drew their weapons at the sailors attempting to reach the flagstaff. The three men were rewarded with a hail of bullets from the mutinous crew; all three died.

There had been rumblings about calls for an end to the monarchy, which would make the royal crown prince an unwelcome sight should he be spotted. Heinrich had to get out. His home had already been invaded by a group of sailors who openly and defiantly insulted him. Fearing there was worse to come, the prince, his wife, and their son disguised themselves by getting into a car with a red flag banner and headed out of the city. As they passed through the crowds, Heinrich could hear people asking each other whether the fleet would still sail, while many others were shouting for an end to the war altogether.

As the family was being driven north, they encountered sailors on the road, who were gathered around a broken-down truck. As they passed, two of the sailors hopped onto the running board of the car as it started to pass them. Although the sailors did not recognize the prince, Heinrich did not know that and immediately feared their intentions. Drawing his pistol, he shot one of the sailors, and immediately, the other jumped off. Another sailor in the group drew his firearm and fired off numerous bullets at the car as it sped by. Finding out that the one who fired on them was the prince, the sailors were incensed. In his hysteria, one sailor screamed, "Treason! Treason! We have been betrayed!" while the other sailors wanted to pursue the royal and bring him to account. Only Noske's purposeful stalling tactics kept the men from their pursuit. The crown prince and his family got away safely, but the incident highlighted the brewing animosity that the monarchy was facing.

Meanwhile, Admiral von Hipper's decision to disperse the navy squadrons along the coast was having the opposite effect he had intended. Instead of separating rebellious sailors and cutting them off from one another, rebellion spread from town to town.

The next few days were a confusing and complex series of events rather than an organized revolution. In Hamburg, sailors marched across the peninsula and began an intensive campaign of propaganda, aiming to draw civilians and garrisoned military troops to their cause. It was highly successful, as was the sailor takeover in Wilhelmshaven and other cities.

Political disruptions also followed. The monarchy in Bavaria fell on November 7th, and the state declared itself a socialist republic. The same day, Munich also declared itself a republic. It seemed that each town and region were participating in revolution in their own way and on their own terms. Yet the capital, Berlin, remained calm—at least on the surface.

But the rumblings of revolution were boiling beneath the surface there as well. Berlin's Revolutionary Stewards, a group of shop owners without an official union, were also looking for an end to the monarchy. Inspired by Russia's Bolshevik Revolution and the protests sweeping through the rest of the country, the Stewards called for their own strike in Berlin and invited others to join them. They would demonstrate in favor of accepting Woodrow Wilson's terms for peace and ending the war. The left-wing Spartacus League gladly jumped at the chance for a potential socialist coup, and it agreed to join in, along with other city unions.

Not to be outdone by their revolutionary counterparts and fearing that they might lose control of some of their members, the Social Democratic Party (SPD) reluctantly agreed to join in at the last minute. It would also be a chance for the party to follow through on the ultimatum they made to Prince Maximilian von Baden on November 7th—either the Kaiser abdicates immediately, or the SPD's ministers would resign from their government positions. When November 9th came around, and the Kaiser was still on the throne, it gave further motivation for the SPD to throw their hat in the ring with the Spartacists and Stewards, even though the party leader, Friedrich Ebert, feared an outbreak of complete revolution or civil war.

That day, Philipp Scheidemann, the deputy chairman of the SPD, declared the onset of the revolution. As armed workers and soldiers began to gather and march that morning, Ebert and von Baden negotiated at the chancellery. Thousands gathered in the city center and occupied police stations, ministries, and other city buildings as the chancellor pushed the Kaiser to abdicate. Wilhelm hesitated. Shots were fired from the crowds of demonstrators, and rather than quell the tumultuous crowd, soldiers joined them. The Kaiser proposed that he lead troops into Berlin and take down the revolutionary throngs. Advisors and field commanders told him it was impossible. The troops could no longer be relied upon to come to the emperor's defense. General Wilhelm Groener put an end to any argument by declaring that "the army will march home in good order under its leaders and commanding generals, but not under the command of Your Majesty, for it stands no longer behind Your Majesty!"

Finally understanding that he had no more military support, the Kaiser proposed that he would abdicate as emperor of Germany but would remain king of Prussia. The one thing the revolutionaries hated more than Wilhelm as emperor was him being the king of Prussia. They considered Wilhelm to be nothing more than a "warlord" over the region. The proposal would also mean that the empire would be broken apart.

Aside from internal pressure, there was international pressure for the dissolution of the monarchy. Woodrow Wilson made the demand for a democratic government in Germany a condition for peace negotiations with the Allies.

Believing that the end of the monarchy was inevitably close at hand and not wanting to delay should the unrest in the city continue to grow, von Baden announced the news that the Kaiser had abdicated. In reality, he had not officially done so, but publishing the statement sealed the Kaiser's fate. In von Baden's next unconstitutional move, he handed over the chancellorship to Ebert. The new chancellor envisioned himself governing a transitional or constitutional monarchy, complete with parliamentary parties, at least for the immediate future until further details could be worked out. But revolutionary leaders had other ideas.

Scheidemann, wanting to beat the communist Spartacists to the punch before they could proclaim Germany a "Soviet Republic," rushed to one of the large windows of Berlin's Reichstag. At 2 p.m., he announced the news to the crowds outside. In a loud voice, he shouted, "Be united, faithful and conscientious. The old and rotten, the monarchy has collapsed. The new may live. Long live the German Republic!"

Although Spartacus League leader Karl Liebknecht was not the first to make the announcement, he was not far behind. Walking onto a balcony at the Stadtschloss at 4 p.m., he proclaimed Germany a free socialist republic.

Though neither proclamation was officially accurate at the time, declaring a socialist republic had not been Ebert's plan, and he was furious about the unsanctioned announcement. However, the course was already set; Ebert could not back out now. With a communist uprising at hand and fear of an extremist takeover hanging in the air, Ebert had little choice but to accept the SPD's declaration. An "accidental republic" had just come into existence.

The same day, workers' and soldiers' councils held a general assembly in Berlin to form and ratify a nationwide Council of People's Representatives. It would form the basis of the provisional government set in place earlier in the day. Two co-chairmen were elected, one from each branch of the Socialist Democratic Party. Ebert was chosen to represent the MSPD. He would now be doing dual duty as chancellor and co-chairman of the council.

Outside in the streets, the revolutionary crowds in Berlin triumphed while largely avoiding violence or other damage. They had helped turn the tide and witnessed the inglorious death of the German Empire and the revolutionary birth of what would soon become the Weimar Republic. But a power struggle would soon erupt.

Chapter 4 – Armistice and Uprising

"Yesterday morning, everything was still there [the Kaiser, the chancellor, the chief of police]; yesterday afternoon nothing of all that existed any longer."–Berliner Tageblatt, November 10th newspaper edition.

Wilhelm II, now former Kaiser of the German Empire, boarded his imperial train bound for Holland. General Paul von Hindenburg had finally convinced him to make his abdication official for the good of the country. They could not negotiate peace with the Allies without such an empire-shaking move. Though Wilhelm would not sign the official act relinquishing his role as emperor of Germany and king of Prussia until November 28th, 1918, he would leave the country in the hands of Friedrich Ebert and the Social Democrats. But the situation was far from stable, and Ebert and the new government remained vulnerable.

Groener, who was still on the Western Front in Belgium, knew this, and he was prepared to make a deal. Late in the evening on November 10th, a phone that Ebert hadn't even known existed rang at the chancellery. It was Groener, calling on a secret line. He was prepared to offer Ebert the loyalty of the military on a few conditions— any leftist Bolshevik uprisings were to be put down immediately, the military was to retain its traditional deep state status under which it was free to operate secretly and independently according to its own goals and agendas, the soldiers' councils were to be disbanded and authority given back to the professional officers' corps, and a national assembly was to be called. Ebert thanked Groener and hung up.

After a series of more calls with Groener, Ebert agreed to the secret pact. Although some would call it a betrayal of the democratic ideals that Ebert held, he had few other options. He was going to need Groener to make good on his promise in the coming months.

The next day, November 11th, the German people got what they had fought and longed for—an end to the Great War. With their troops still on foreign soil and a provisional democratic government newly born, German officials went to Rethondes, France, to meet with Allied generals.

Although ending the war was a triumphant event, the terms that Germany had to agree to were severe. The Allies wanted to ensure that Germany would not continue the fight, little realizing that, with its navy in shambles, there was little chance that it could at the moment. The German army was also in retreat, and its entire left flank was about to be routed by Allies poised to strike. Still, the Germans had to agree to complete demilitarization, as well as the full withdrawal of its troops from France, Belgium, and the territory of Alsace-Lorraine. They were also to release all Allied prisoners of war immediately. Germany had little choice but to agree, and the armistice was signed.

Aside from ending the disastrous war, the armistice did little to relieve Germany. It remained on the verge of total collapse. The Spanish flu swept through Europe and ravaged people who were already on the cusp of starvation. The Allied blockade continued after the war was over, preventing Germans from getting much-needed food, fuel, and other necessities. Soldiers returning from the war were faced with conditions no better than when they had left. Hundreds of thousands of men came home jobless, hungry, disillusioned, and bitter—the main ingredients for revolution.

In a political sense, Germany's future also remained highly uncertain. Ebert and his majority Social Democratic Party had taken control of the government, but keeping order remained elusive. His first act as chancellor had been to call for peace and for people to get off the streets so order could be restored. It did not work.

With various parties vying for power, confusion instead of peace resulted. Radicals, workers' and soldiers' councils, and other political parties (such as the Independents) sought to overtake the government and implement their own plans for the rule. Revolutionary movements continued, with various groups overtaking city halls and state government buildings around the country.

One of the most radical of these groups was the Spartacus League. Enamored with the Bolshevik leadership newly taken hold in Russia, League leaders Karl Liebknecht and Rosa Luxemburg sought to turn the country into a republic run by workers' and soldiers' councils. They believed that the Bolshevik Revolution that had spread through Russia would make its way to Germany and be heartily embraced by the people. Liebknecht envisioned himself as the German version of Vladimir Lenin, and much to his chagrin, Ebert was now forced to share power with him and his party.

The plot the Spartacists were brewing came into action in January of 1919. Or at least it was attempted. Looking for a reason to protest, calls for a general strike and demonstrations against the dismissal of Berlin Police Chief Robert Emil Eichhorn were instigated by the

Revolutionary Stewards and set for January 5th, 1919. Their call produced quite a turnout—500,000 people massed together in protest in Berlin, a surprise even to the leaders of the demonstration. A disenfranchised Eichhorn helped to provide weapons to those who showed up. It wasn't long before armed protesters began to seize important buildings around the city, such as Berlin newspaper editorial offices, train stations, and other media buildings.

But the true intentions of the Stewards and the Spartacus League became apparent in a meeting between several parties at the Berlin police station—they called for an overthrow of Ebert's government. Those in attendance, including Liebknecht and Eichhorn, overwhelmingly agreed to the proposal in an 80 to 6 vote. They thereafter declared the government had been taken over on their order. But those words proved to be empty without the ability to carry it out.

The rebels couldn't agree on what to do next. Some wanted to enter into talks with Ebert, while others favored armed insurrection. But that would require the help of the military. In their first fatal mistake, they had overestimated and banked on the support of the military in Berlin, and attempts to garner that support failed epically.

With no further action able to be taken that day, they called for more worker demonstrations on January 6th. But in their second critical error, the radicals had seriously miscalculated the mood of the people, particularly German workers. They were not as poised for revolution as the Spartacists had believed. Instead of warmly welcoming the Bolshevik communism that Liebknecht and Luxemburg thought would take root, many preferred Ebert's moderate and democratic approach to socialism and remained loyal to the government's majority party. This was reinforced in response to the government's call for help. Factories emptied, and an opposing force of workers met the revolutionary demonstrators, creating a human wall and blocking them from marching into government buildings.

Despite the fact that the revolutionaries were armed and the factory workers supporting the government were not, there was a calm among the crowd. Only a few radicals fought around the city. This perplexed the revolutionary leaders. By that night, Liebknecht and Luxemburg saw the hopelessness of the action they had started the day before. With little choice left, mediation between the government and revolting parties was agreed to, and the crowds outside largely dispersed. But the trouble was not over yet.

Back in December, Noske was tasked with a secret training assignment. Taking soldiers returning from the front and some civilian volunteers, he trained the men and formed a volunteer militia with the wink and nod of the government. The men, who were still primed for war but having none to fight, readily formed groups with charismatic former officers at their core. These Freikorps ("Free Corps"), as they came to be called, were now called upon to protect Berlin.

On January 11th, Noske and two thousand Freikorps troops marched into Berlin, expecting resistance. Instead, they were met with widespread applause. But in pockets around the city, rebels, although now greatly reduced, still fought in some key areas of the city. Armed with artillery, grenades, and machine guns, the Freikorps took back government buildings, police headquarters, and publishing offices under Spartacist control. Far from bloodless, the intense struggle ended with at least 165 demonstrators shot dead, some after they had already tried to surrender to the militia.

Luxemburg and Liebknecht had completely lost control of the situation. Resigning himself to defeat, Liebknecht declared, "Ultimately one should accept history as it develops." But historical developments would not show any favor to the revolutionary leaders.

Not wanting to leave their fate to chance, the two took up hiding in the house of friends. But only a few days later, on January 15th, Freikorps units came through their door. The two were taken to the Hotel Eden, where both ended up dead. The official story of their deaths reported that Liebknecht was shot while trying to escape and that Luxemburg was killed by an angry mob. In reality, though, Liebknecht was shot by the soldiers at the hotel. Luxemburg suffered her death with the butt of a rifle, after which she was shot. One of the soldiers who helped throw her body in the Landwehr Canal looked down into the water and remarked, "The old slut is swimming now."

Sporadic revolutionary movements continued around Germany in the months that followed, but they, too, proved weak and ineffectual. Groener's regular army, with the help of the Freikorps, continued to suppress the revolution, including an uprising in Bavaria. But despite the pockets of rebellion, the failure of the movement in Berlin had already doomed the fate of the revolution—it had lost all legitimacy. On January 19th, the elections that the Spartacists had fought to stop took place. Overwhelmingly, the vote was for democracy. Ebert could celebrate, as his vision for German democracy was becoming a reality.

On February 9th, the Weimar National Assembly came together to begin establishing the democratic republic. But given the uprisings of the last several months, holding the assembly in one of the government buildings in Berlin would have been foolishly risky. Instead, the small city of Weimar was chosen, a haven far removed from the radical activities to which Berlin was susceptible.

While the new republic was being built in Weimar, international deliberations over Germany's fate were being hotly debated by the Allies.

Chapter 5 – One of the Most Hated Treaties in History

The painting of Louis XIV stared out from the center of the hall. He presided over the numerous long tables placed among the opulent Hall of Mirrors in the "hunting lodge" his family had built more than two centuries earlier. Thousands of tiny crystals from the glamorous chandeliers above reflected light coming in from the floor-to-ceiling windows looking out over the well-manicured gardens.

Beneath the sculptured gold-laden ceiling were chairs occupied by the twenty-seven delegates sent from thirty-two countries. But with clerks, assistants, and the press, there were about two thousand people in the room. The solemn occasion was a far cry from the music and dancing that the hall had originally been intended for. The documents to formally end World War I had been laid out, awaiting signatures from Hermann Müller and Johannes Bell.

Months earlier, the drafting of the treaty had begun in Paris. The path to negotiating peace proved to be a difficult one, even among the Allies. Before they had even reached the negotiating table, disagreements arose about where to hold the conference. The British argued that given the animosity the French held toward Germany, the peace conference should not be held in Paris. The French would not hear of it—they demanded the conference as part of what they were owed for their immense suffering during the war. The others could not see fit to deny them this. And so, on January 18th, the assembly gathered to begin the drafting process.

The trouble was, each country had its own complaints and agendas to address. And unbeknownst to the Americans, some of the Europeans had secret treaties and territorial claims in play, further complicating the matter. So, creating a seamless document from, at times, contradictory opinions was no easy task. But most notably, Germany was not asked for its opinion or input—it had been decidedly excluded from the negotiation process.

France wanted revenge and reparations and to ensure the German threat was permanently removed, while the US, under Woodrow Wilson's Fourteen Points, dreamed of world peace. The British were somewhere in between; they were also looking for reparations but took a more moderate stance that compromised on the US agenda. Meanwhile, Italy sought to claim territories that it was supposed to take over in 1915. These were just the agendas of the "Big Four"— there were other countries who wanted a say as well.

Understandable, France's security was a prime concern for their prime minister, Georges Clemenceau. Numerous times over the past one hundred years, starting with the invasion in 1814, German forces had swept their way into France. France was determined that it would never happen again. And not only that, but it also wanted Germany to pay reparations for the damage done to the country—an astounding figure to the tune of twenty billion gold marks.

Britain had not suffered as much as France, but 900,000 of her people were killed, and over two million were injured. The state of its soldiers coming from German prisoner of war camps also painted a grim picture of what the British had suffered. When one nineteen-year-old soldier came back from the Friedrichsfeld prisoner camp, he weighed only fifty-six pounds and was riddled with lice and tuberculosis. This had whipped the British public into a frenzy when they heard about it. Sir Eric Geddes proclaimed that the government would squeeze Germany "'til the pips squeaked," while the people of London called to hang the Kaiser—they clamored for blood.

British Prime Minister David Lloyd George knew that justice demanded Germany indemnify Britain for the "destruction her criminal aggression had caused," but he also knew that the German coffers had been bled dry by the war. There was no gold left in the treasury, and if Germany tried to print more money to pay, it would be rendered virtually worthless. Lloyd George was well aware of the alternative that Germany would attempt to turn to—giving other countries industrial goods they produced in lieu of money. Lloyd George firmly stated, "Whatever happens, Germany is not to pay the indemnity by merely dumping cheap German goods upon other countries. She ought to pay, she must pay as far as she can, but we are not going to allow her to pay in such a way as to wreck our industries."

But disturbing reports that the German people were on the brink of starvation reached the Americans and Brits. British troops in Germany were affected as well, facing starvation themselves due to the lack of food in the country. Starving Germany's populace hadn't been the goal of the United States and Britain, but a difference in attitudes among the Allies caused a rift. After the devastation Germany had caused, after the multitude of vicious atrocities the German army had committed, it was hard for France to care whether the people there starved. Belgium had fared little better, as unimaginable savagery ripped apart the country that had declared itself neutral. They, too, found it hard to muster sympathy for the starving German people.

Wilson called for "open covenants of peace, openly arrived at." The other countries looked upon him with contempt, feeling that his calls for peace were naïve and that he was taking on an air of superiority. Still, he pushed for the treaty to be based on his Fourteen Points.

Many of the points required concessions from other countries, including Britain and France. Though the other Allies could appreciate how Wilson's points helped to end the war, they felt that they didn't reflect the sympathy they deserved given their own devastation. It was a devastation that had not personally affected Americans in their own country, and as such, they did not understand. To them, Wilson's points felt, as Edmund Burke put it, "the cold neutrality of an impartial judge." However, Wilson insisted. The Allies pushed back. They had doubts about Wilson's claims that he spoke for the peace of humanity. They wanted an agreement in which Germany would pay dearly and one in which they had little to sacrifice by way of compromise.

The powers met on January 12th at the foreign minister's office on Quai d'Orsay. Though the meeting opened with reports on German compliance with the armistice, stories of Germans' ill-treatment and even deliberate killing of prisoners were soon brought up. The British became incensed at this. David Lloyd George made an angry declaration, saying, "We must obtain justice for this!"

It was a serious accusation leveled against the Germans. Wilson, although sickened by the knowledge that the stories were likely true, asked if there was evidence to back up the claims. An interpreter was handed the reports to read to Wilson. Within just a few paragraphs, so many terrible words and phrases were left hanging in the air. "Shot in the back...starved...beaten...machine-gunned." Wilson had heard enough. Nauseated, he held up his hand for the interpreter to stop reading.

The next day, the question of sending food to a starving Germany was raised. The Allies were obligated to do so under the terms of the armistice, but yet there was reluctance. The food issue was proposed as a priority over enforcing Germany's debt obligations. France was immediately angered by the proposal, still reeling under the weight of her losses. Though none of the lives lost could be quantified or returned by Germany paying money, the French bristled at the thought of now feeding those who caused them so much pain and harm. Given the intensity of the feelings involved, the matter had to be set aside for the time being.

With feelings so very raw, the atmosphere became more and more intense as negotiations went on. At one point, Wilson threatened to walk out of the council. Italian Prime Minister Vittorio Orlando suffered a nervous collapse and had to leave for a time in order to recover. British Prime Minister David Lloyd George and French Prime Minister Georges Clemenceau nearly came to blows; a fistfight was only prevented because Wilson stepped in between them.

In April, a German delegation was finally invited to come to Paris. But if they had notions of being welcomed as members of a fledgling democracy, they were sorely disappointed. Germany was still viewed as a pariah, and its representatives were forced to face fresh resentments directed at them by leaders of the other countries.

On May 7th, 1919, the final version of the treaty was presented to the German representatives. Although Wilson had pushed for fair and conciliatory terms for Germany, the conditions finally agreed upon were absolutely punishing. Though the Germans had somewhat expected this, the agreement was beyond what they had anticipated. It was a hard pill to swallow for the newly elected government that had not started the war but were now left to clean up and navigate the peace process.

Besides being required to pay reparations, Germany had to give up territory, which meant a loss for their ore and agricultural production. The country's foreign financial holdings would be confiscated, and commercial contracts with other countries were to be canceled. It would be a catastrophic blow to the German economy.

Germany would need to reduce its military to no more than 100,000 men, get rid of all military aircraft, and limit any future munitions-building. Their ailing military would be further crippled by these conditions. In addition, those listed as war criminals by the Allies were to be handed over for trial, including the former emperor.

In a final blow to their honor, the Germans were also compelled to agree to take sole blame for the war. The representatives from Germany complained bitterly, though their complaints fell on deaf ears.

Even more so, the response from the German people was a unanimous outcry. No matter what political party a person belonged to, all could agree that the terms of the treaty were too much. It was bad enough that the treaty barred them from joining the newly formed League of Nations, but this was more than their dignity could bear. The people, as well as government officials, protested and strongly opposed the agreement. They accused the Allies of egregiously violating the very principles of peace Wilson had set out. The Germans would not sign.

The agreement sent the newly established provisional government in Weimar into a complete uproar. The tenuous political situation went into upheaval. Upon reading the terms, Scheidemann exclaimed, "What hand would not wither that binds itself and us in these fetters?" Refusing to sign the agreement, he stepped down from his position. Von Hindenburg also resigned, declaring the army was in no position to fight even if it wanted to.

But despite their protestations, Germany did not have a leg to stand on. It would have to agree to the terms without negotiation. The Allies were presenting the agreement on a take it or leave it basis, and if the Germans left it, there would be severe consequences. When June came and the treaty had not been confirmed by the Germans, the Allies issued an ultimatum—sign it or expect an Allied invasion. Groener, seeing the futility and potential catastrophe of continuing to fight the Allies, urged the government to accept the treaty.

On June 28th, exactly five years after Archduke Franz Ferdinand was assassinated, the murder that had sparked the war, German and Allied representatives met in the Palace of Versailles to sign the treaty. Perhaps in a stroke of poetic justice, the Hall of Mirrors, the place where the documents were now to be signed, was the very place where

Germany had stood and proclaimed its empire in 1871. The mood of the Germans was vastly different now.

Solemnly, Müller and Bell walked into the hall, following the Allied representatives, paled and with their eyes fixed above, avoiding the stares of two thousand glaring attendees. After a few words from Clemenceau, the men were led with dignity to the small table containing the treaty. Germany would be the first to sign as silence came over the hall.

When the document was signed by the two Germans, everyone in the room let out a collective breath, and an air of relaxation took over. Outside, guns thundered a salute and announced to the city that Germany had signed. Through the open windows, crowds could be heard cheering.

For three hours, delegates came up to the table and signed. Once it was done, Sir Harold Nicolson, a member of the British delegation, noted that everyone in the room stayed seated and silent as "the Germans were conducted like prisoners from the dock, their eyes still fixed upon some distant point of the horizon."

Though the treaty had now come into force, it was disliked by every nation that signed it. It seemed that nobody truly got what they wanted out of it, and it would leave Germany further decimated and seething for revenge. The Treaty of Versailles became known as one of history's most hated treaties. The call for peace had become more about punishing the past than rebuilding for the future. Or rather, it could be stated for rebuilding a peaceful future: the treaty did lay the foundation going forward, one with more terrible consequences and one that would lead to a second world war.

Chapter 6 – The Weimar Republic Becomes a Constitutional and Democratic Government

While the Allies had been hotly debating the terms of the treaty, politicians, scholars, and other prominent Germans, twenty-five men in all, worked on drafting Weimar's new constitution. With radical left- and right-wing political parties and everyone in between to appease, the men had an unenviably difficult task ahead of them—creating a government that all could be happy with.

Finally, on August 11th, 1919, it was drafted into law. It had taken four readthroughs and some major changes to come to a final document, but the constitution that was put into effect was lauded as "the most modern democratic constitution of its day." The new democratic system had now effectively put an end to the socialist republic that Scheidemann had so brazenly and dramatically announced months earlier.

On the surface, it bore some resemblance to the democratic system of the United States, but there were also many differences between American and German democracy. The country was to have a democratically elected president who would hold real power—including total control over the military and the ability to call for new parliamentary elections—for a seven-year term. Worried about a resurgence of the monarchy, Social Democrats insisted that the constitution deem any members of former imperial dynasties ineligible for the presidency.

The new government would also include a chancellor selected from the majority party (or a majority coalition if no majority party existed) by the president, and his chosen cabinet would be responsible for the day-to-day aspects of running the government. The chancellor would also be obligated to endorse all orders set out by the president.

There was also to be a parliament (Reichstag), and the representatives of the people would be elected every four years by popular vote. The number of representatives from each state would be proportional to its size and population. Those elected were essentially guardians of Germany's democracy.

The constitution officially afforded all Germans basic civil rights and responsibilities. They were allowed freedoms such as that of expression, peaceful assembly, and religion, as well as the rights to public education for children, to own property, and equal opportunities for employment and wages—this last one had been a major point of contention among the workers who protested for many years.

For the first time in their history, the German people would have a voice and a say in their own government. But democracy was not without its pitfalls. For one, the system allowed for an abundance of political parties to crop up and have representation. Oftentimes, competing agendas and interests made it difficult to gain a majority vote or form a majority governing coalition. For instance, there were niche parties like the Bavarian Peasants' League, a group whose sole focus was on agricultural interests in that part of the county. With .8 percent of the vote, they only had four seats in parliament, representing just a small and very specific fraction of the population. But the system of proportional representation would provide an opportunity for bigger problems to emerge in the future, namely opening the way for extremist political parties to take hold and tighten their grip.

The Weimar Constitution contained a total of 181 articles, but there was one that became highly controversial. Article 48, born out of conservative party fears of too much democracy, gave the president power that others found unsettling. Absolute power could be exercised if the president felt it necessary to intervene if a state was not living up to its duties toward the constitution or federal laws. In cases of major threats to public safety (such as the previous mutinies and protests), the president could temporarily suspend certain civil rights in the interest of restoring order.

But the framers tried to ensure that these dictatorial powers did not come without some checks and balances. Any actions the president took under this article technically had to be run by parliament, which, if they deemed fit, could demand the ordinances be lifted. In this way, the constitution essentially allowed parliament control over presidential actions, with the aim of strengthening and protecting the democracy it promised.

However, there was still a provision for the president to act without the consent of parliament for limited periods. Ebert later used the article to remedy emergency situations where political parties couldn't agree or were too slow to act. This, in and of itself, was not bad; in fact, the use of Article 48 was necessary and helpful, but it set a dangerous precedent.

The political parties comprising the government were now thrown into a role of serious responsibility—a role for which they were not fully equipped or prepared. More than that, there was doubt whether those political parties even wanted the responsibility. They fought to have power and a say, but when it came down to it, as German historian and political economist Max Weber stated, many did not want to face realities and the compromises and decisions that would have to be made.

This is where the dangerous precedent set by Article 48 came into play during the following years. It was felt that those within governing political parties could dismiss and neglect legislative duties that they found unpleasant because they knew that, under Article 48, there was another power capable of dealing with them. So, if a particular duty didn't suit them, they felt no conscience about leaving it to someone else, knowing that the president had the power to take over the responsibility.

Having a president now made it easy for those who wanted power to retain it while allowing them to shirk their responsibilities. This made the government, in some ways, more of a façade of democracy than a smoothly functioning system. Ultimately, this lack of accountability would lead to the republic's demise.

Chapter 7 – The Kapp Putsch

For the German people, the humiliation of the treaty was still fresh, and its sting continued to be felt among the nation. Being forced to take the blame for the entire war (a term that they did not agree with), saddled with crippling reparations, and being insulted by not even having been allowed to take part in the drafting of the treaty that had such drastic effects on the whole country was bad enough. The treaty did nothing to repair relations with France, as its troops continued to occupy the Rhineland in order to create a secure buffer in case Germany decided to attempt another invasion. The Germans saw this as an inflexible hostility on the part of the French.

But the people also felt betrayed by their own government. A myth started by some in the military that said Germany had not actually been defeated, and the tale was soon whispered around the country. The idea that instead of being defeated, the country had been stabbed in the back by "the November criminals"—republicans, socialists, and even Jews who supported signing the treaty—continued to be insidiously spread by enemies of the newly established republic. Even though there was no other reasonable choice, the leaders responsible for signing the peace were now vilified as traitors to their nation. Resentments simmered.

One of those who held such angry resentments over this perceived humiliation was Wolfgang Kapp, a right-wing Prussian politician vehemently opposed to Ebert and everything for which his government stood. Kapp made it his aim to oust Ebert and his cabinet in order to install a right-wing dictatorship over the land.

Many in the military shared Kapp's view that leftist politics had led to the collapse of the Second Reich. In particular, Kapp found an ally in the commanding general of Germany's army, Walter von Lüttwitz, whose main agenda was to flout certain articles in the Treaty of Versailles, including those that put a cap on the country's army. Lüttwitz was already instigating plans against Ebert and would gladly take Kapp's assistance.

After months of plotting, the time to act came on Friday, March 12th, 1920. Lüttwitz's army, along with some Freikorps troops, marched toward Berlin. By 6 a.m. Saturday morning, they entered the city. Wanting to avoid panic and chaos, commanders gave specific instructions to troops to maintain control and order. Troops seized strategically advantageous positions around the city and set up machine guns and posted signs with an ominous warning—"Whoever proceeds will be shot!"

Fear of Kapp caused a curious reaction among Berliners. They tried to avoid violence, and there was an incredible show of goodwill toward the marching army. Black, white, and red flags proudly hung in windows, while others threw flowers at soldiers as they passed. Stunt planes performed overhead, giving the city an air of celebration. That façade would not last long.

As soldiers took over government buildings around Berlin, the mood of the people turned sour. Workers in the city did not even try to disguise their contempt for what was happening. Faces remained somber, and workers muttered among themselves. Some used what was happening to neglect their jobs.

Ebert and his cabinet were not naïve about what was happening. They knew what an attempted coup would mean for them. Their best chance at stopping it was to flee the city and remain free to organize a counter-resistance.

As the government fled the city, Kapp prepared to make his grand proclamation of a takeover. Perhaps expecting the help of the press office, Kapp soon found that making his announcement would not be easy. The press chief, Herr Schnitzler, as well as typists (along with their typewriters), were nowhere to be found. Those who did remain refused to prepare the manifesto for publication and had "conveniently" changed the deadline for publishing submissions.

When Kapp finally got his proclamation printed on leaflets, they were dropped from planes and handed out by soldiers. For the most part, Berliners went about their daily lives, almost completely ignoring the information on the leaflets.

As Kapp tried to quickly fill cabinet positions to give his regime an air of legitimacy, he ran into more obstacles. He found it difficult to find those who would support his scheme and were willing to fill those governmental positions. Bureaucratic ministers who had remained refused to cooperate with Kapp.

President Ebert finally reached a safe location, and he sent a message to the people. He knew that if he couldn't get the full military support he would need, he would have to encourage the people themselves to rise up and fight those trying to overthrow their legitimate government. But instead of calling for violence, Ebert used strategy. He and other leading members of the government urged for a general strike. Calling on their loyalty to the republic, Ebert sent his appeal out to workers around the entire country. "Strike! Lay down your work and strangle this military dictatorship! Fight with every weapon to preserve the Republic! Lay aside every division. There is but one means to achieve this goal: the paralysis of all economic life. Not a hand must stir, not a worker give aid to the military dictatorship. General strike all along the line! Proletarians, unite!"

Ebert's call was answered. Despite the deep divide they suffered among themselves, the German trade unions and other workers' organizations banded together for a common cause. Only essential workers, such as those taking care of the water systems and hospital workers, were exempted from duty.

On March 14th, the nationwide strike was officially launched. Many workers had already walked out of their jobs the day before; in fact, some factories had shuttered their doors by noon the day before.

That same morning, the two pro-government newspapers in Berlin were taken over by revolutionary forces. Without delay, every printer in the city walked out of their offices and joined the strike. Telegraph operators at the city post office stood against the Kappist regime, refusing to yield to its demands.

Though there was a mixed reaction to the coup by the military, one thing was becoming abundantly clear—the German people were not behind the coup and the new regime it sought to impose. The workers' strike had become nearly universal. Hotels and restaurants closed. The strikes escalated over time, and with no one to operate city services like trains, gas, electricity, water, telegraph services, or newspapers, the city went dark, and communication was lacking. Kapp and his followers were hard-pressed to continue their operations.

Without the help of the telegraph clerks, Kappists had no choice but to take over themselves. In this way, they could control the information coming and going from the city. They kept a tight grip on it, as only messages that they approved could be sent. Of course, any news of the workers' opposition to the Kappist occupation was certainly not among them.

This did not stop the telegraph clerks, however. Disregarding the press censorship that had been set up, correspondents refused to submit their dispatches for approval. Instead, they used various ingenious means to get around the censors and send their messages through. Newspaper editors also used some creativity to circumvent censors who would not allow Berlin papers to run. Instead of paper, they printed the news on placards and displayed them in the windows of the numerous press agencies around the city.

The Kappists had another problem to face—being able to access the money they desperately needed. The state bank refused to give into successive attempts by the Kappists to obtain funds, as bank officials refused to sign the forms needed to release them. The Kappist leaders became exasperated by this new obstacle. If the bank would not willingly hand over the money, they would just take it. However, the representatives they sent refused to do so, not wanting to become literal bank robbers.

The Kappists' tenuous grasp was quickly slipping. The only thing keeping them in power was the support of the military, but they would need the support of the workers as well. Some called for negotiations. Others called for an iron fist. The attempts they had already made to use brute force to intimidate and overwhelm workers and the general public had apparently failed. If they were to be taken seriously, there would need to be something more drastic to capture the attention and allegiance of the people, particularly the strikers.

So, on March 15th, another proclamation was sent out, this one with a more ominous tone. In a dire message to striking workers and their leaders, it warned that "the ringleaders who are guilty of acts specified in the degree for safe-guarding important economic services, and in the decree for the protection of labor peace, as well as the strike pickets, will be punished with death."

But the workers would not be cowed by threatening messages from a regime they refused to recognize. Instead of halting the strikes, the Kappist message seemed to have the opposite effect—it galvanized workers across the country, and more and more went on strike. Industry in the Ruhr region came to an abrupt standstill. Barbed wire was set up around railroad stations as the entire system ground to a halt. Communications systems were virtually paralyzed, and when the Technical Emergency Corps tried to restore water, electricity, and other basic services, they were met with fierce resistance from the people.

The lack of cooperation from bureaucrats and the populace began to spell doom for the ailing coup. Putsch leaders began to fear that they would not be able to maintain control over the country. With their last decree to strikers largely ignored, some Kappists called for even more brutal measures to be taken.

Soldiers had already set up barbed wire barriers on the main streets of Berlin and engaged in violent clashes with protesters, opening fire and killing or wounding several. Protesters in other cities like Frankfurt also engaged soldiers in violent confrontations. With the Kappists' previous warning having lacked in effectiveness, it was suggested that picketers and trade union leaders be shot down in cold blood, making them an example. They hoped this precedent would show that the Kappists' threats were serious and carried weight, thereby scaring workers into going back to their jobs lest they suffer the same fate.

However, Kapp and Lüttwitz put this suggestion in check. How could they send armed troops to shoot largely unarmed and non-violently protesting German citizens? Military support for the regime was already quickly ebbing, so it was unlikely that they would support action that would amount to assassinations and the massacre of their own people. Hope was quickly being lost in all corners of the coup.

After Ebert's urgent call for workers to strike, he and his government did not sit idly by as Kappists struggled in Berlin. Capitalizing on the Kappists' weakening stance, Ebert's government sent a plane to drop leaflets over the capital on March 16th. The foreboding title was a portentous message against the Kappist coup. It announced, "The Collapse of the Military Dictatorship." And how predictive it was.

Kapp and other putsch leaders frantically sought a solution to prevent the demise of their government. In a desperate attempt, Kapp reached out to Ebert's government and offered them a compromise.

The most notable of the terms was that both governments would condemn the strikes and urge the people to go back to work. Ebert found this almost laughable, and in no uncertain terms, he refused to even consider Kapp's words.

Having failed to strike a compromise, Kapp's desperation led to another wild scheme. In an effort to distract the people and divert attention from themselves, Kappists endeavored to drum up anti-Jewish sentiments among the people. To accomplish this, they handed out leaflets that stated flour reserved for use during the Jewish Passover had been seized by the regime and would be graciously distributed to workers. This play to gain control over the population failed miserably. Options were running out.

The military battalion that had marched into Berlin with Kapp and Lüttwitz mutinied. Soldiers arrested their commanding officers and afterward pledged their allegiance to the rightful constitutional government. The next day, the Berlin Security Police followed suit, not only announcing loyalty to Ebert's government but also demanding a full Kappist resignation. Clashes in the city streets ramped up, and casualties mounted.

It was becoming abundantly clear that the Kappists had virtually no support within the entire country. So, they turned to the international scene. But their hope for foreign support was quickly dashed by a message from British officials. They notified Kapp that Great Britain refused to recognize the legitimacy of his government and that they would not find support from their corner. These were the final nails in Kapp's coffin.

Kapp knew it was time to go. But Lüttwitz was not quite ready to give up the reins, and he briefly considered setting himself up as a military dictator over the country. But it was obvious that this, too, would prove futile. Kapp drafted his resignation.

A mere five very eventful days after it began, the Kappist government fell at 6 p.m. on March 17th. As Kapp and Lüttwitz fled from Berlin, they left behind confusion. Scared soldiers, who had been abandoned by the regime they had supported, fought with armed workers around the country for a number of days. Ebert and his government returned to Berlin, having learned two important lessons in the hardest of ways—the Weimar government did not have universal support from the military, and Ebert could not take their support for granted. Secondly, the coup revealed a weakness within the government, showing that its ability to quell uprisings was limited and, by extension, that the safety of the politicians in Berlin could not be guaranteed.

However, Ebert's return restored some semblance of peace. He and his cabinet reestablished themselves quickly and were up and running again by March 27th. But the events of March 17th had not stopped the strikers' momentum. Though Ebert restored general order, the long-simmering economic demands of the workers had not been resolved.

Chapter 8 – The Misery of Hyperinflation and a Crumbling Economy

"The printing presses of the government could no longer keep pace...You could see mail-carriers on the streets with sacks on their backs or pushing baby carriages before them, loaded with paper money that would be devalued the next day. Life was madness, nightmare, desperation, chaos...Communities printed their own money, based on goods...Shoe factories paid their workers in bonds for shoes which they could exchange at the bakery for bread or the meat market for meat."–Konrad Heiden, German eyewitness

Before the war, the country's leaders felt secure in the empire's wealth. But they wanted more. They had dreams of a quick war in which they would afterward reap the bounty of war indemnities from the countries they defeated. Banking on this, they felt justified taking outrageous financial liberties.

With German coffers rapidly running dry during a war that was not as quick to end in victory as people had anticipated, economic troubles loomed. Further complicating the matter was the closing of stock exchanges in Germany and other countries. In order to hide this growing financial problem from the people while still pulling in the money it needed to fund the war, the government called on the nation's patriotism. They encouraged people to contribute with patriotic slogans like "I gave iron for gold" and "Invest in war loans."

However, it was hard to continue to hide the effects as prices rose and the standard of living declined. Soldiers deserted the German military in droves, motivated by the poverty facing their families. After the war, soldiers discharged from their duties returned home, flooding the market with men in search of work. Unemployment took a hard toll on many.

As the insolvent country became burdened with outrageous reparations that it had no reasonable way of paying, it also struggled to find a revenue replacement for the mines and agricultural regions that had been parceled out in the terms of the treaty. The economic situation bordered on catastrophic. And now, after the nationwide strikes prompted by the Kapp Putsch, which shut down mines, factories, and other industries necessary to keep the economy functioning, the Weimar financial situation slid further into the abyss.

The reality of those prewar dreams of economic prosperity had now become a hyperinflation horror story. The country was hardly even recognizable, having changed so drastically within a few years. To those living through it, they had never foreseen this outcome, and the situation remained unpredictable.

Now, Germany faced another conundrum. Besides the immensity of reparations due, there was the fact that the Allies insisted that it could only be paid in gold or foreign currency. The trouble was, there was no gold left in the treasury. The only other option was foreign currency. The government scrambled to use German currency to buy foreign money. And when the German currency ran out, the federal government simply printed more. It would prove to be a short-sighted and disastrous move.

As markets became flooded with German marks, its value plummeted. As the value plummeted, more marks were printed in order to continue buying foreign currency. And so it became a vicious cycle until the German mark became virtually worthless. Buying foreign currency was nearly impossible. The only thing Germany had left to pay in terms of the reparations was coal and other goods, strangling the supply of those things within the country.

Hyperinflation rampaged at breakneck speed, becoming like a runaway train. Prices for goods skyrocketed. Whereas in 1919, a loaf of bread had cost one mark, in 1922, it cost a staggering one hundred billion marks. The cost of living became almost prohibitive for the average person, and they began to lose everything they had. Those who had been comfortably in the middle class were now finding themselves completely destitute.

When the people began to realize that the value of their money was free-falling, they raced to spend it while it still had some worth. This created yet another vicious cycle—the faster the people spent their money, the faster prices for goods jumped.

With few choices available, people set up a "bartering economy" in order to get basic necessities. Those who could not barter were forced to turn to less savory methods. One economic expert revealed that "the law-abiding country crumbled into petty thievery." Looting took place under the noses of overwhelmed police forces.

The rise in costs did not just affect citizens; the ripple effect of hyperinflation was felt by the Weimar government. When the prices of goods rose, so did the operating costs of the government. With their assets already bleeding toward buying foreign currency for reparations, there was little left for goods and operations. They were now in a serious bind.

If the government raised taxes, they would be paid in the rapidly devaluing German currency. The money would be as worthless to them as it was to the people who paid it. Besides printing more money, the government tried to issue bonds, but that also served to reduce the value of the currency.

Having no other political allies, Germany turned toward Russia. With Russia also in an isolationist situation, the Weimar government was banking on the country having sympathy for their similar situations. They also had another common interest—Poland.

In 1920, Germany created an economic blockade of Poland, but it quickly failed. Heavy losses to German businessmen due to the failure only served to further weaken the Weimar Republic's economic situation. Thus, closer cooperation with Russia was proposed.

Even though Russia had no claim to the territory and Germany had to renounce it in the treaty (even though they actually never agreed to recognize the German-Poland border anyway), both felt that the industries and resources there could be a viable option for market opportunities and therefore financial relief. If they banded together, perhaps they could claim certain parts of Poland for themselves.

On April 16th, 1922, Germany and Russia secretly signed the Treaty of Rapallo. They not only renounced territorial claims against each other but also canceled financial debts toward each other, relieving some of the foreign financial responsibilities weighing heavily on the Weimar government. Both countries also possessed the human resources the other needed to succeed. Cooperation could lead to a successful symbiotic relationship between the countries. But first, Germany was compelled to recognize the Soviet Bolshevik government as the only legitimate government in Russia.

Despite the agreement, Weimar's economic disaster persisted, and options were running short. If inflation continued its skyward trajectory, Germany would not be able to pay its foreign debt, putting them in violation of the treaty's terms. Yet if they curbed inflation, the immediate effects would be catastrophic. Bankruptcies and unemployment would surely be followed by starvation and strikes. And as the situation quickly became desperate, hunger and strikes would turn into violence, civil disorder, and insurrection. The possibility of revolution would then be at an all-time high.

The Weimar government came to the realization that it could not pay for reparations and pull the country from the brink of starvation and violence at the same time. In 1922, German officials asked the Allies for a temporary suspension of reparation payments to allow the economy to recover. The Allies refused. By 1923, the Weimar economy had reached a breaking point, and Germany had no choice but to stop paying reparations.

France and Belgium, in particular, became incensed. They did not believe that Germany was unable to repay. And they were going to get their money one way or another. Not caring about what the League of Nations charter had to say on the matter, France and Belgium marched into Germany's Ruhr region on January 9th, 1923. It was by all accounts an illegal invasion and occupation, and it was a blatant violation of international terms.

However, they were not interested in gaining territory. The industry-heavy Ruhr region, with its many factories and other resources like timber, coal, iron, and steel, was strategic for France and Belgium in recouping their reparations. They would take what was owed them from the country's industry.

The German people were outraged by this. Industrialists, with the blessing and backing of the government, organized a passive resistance in response to the invasion. Workers were ordered to do nothing that would help France or Belgium in any way. And since those countries were interested in the goods produced and resources being mined, the only way the workers could truly resist was through a general strike.

France and Belgium were undeterred. To solve the problem, they sent in their own workers. Still, the French and Belgians were angered by the strike. They retaliated by arresting strike leaders and members of the German police. Violent clashes ensued. In the next eight months, 132 people would be dead from the encounters, and 150,000 Ruhr citizens would be driven from their homes.

Though the German workers were striking in solidarity with their government, they still had to feed themselves and their families. The government felt responsible and gave them financial support and paid their wages while they continued the strike. Those who lost their homes also needed to be cared for. The trouble was, the government's finances were already stretched too thin. They resolved this by printing even more money. In consequence, more currency flooded the market, further exacerbating the hyperinflation issue.

When other countries saw that Germany's solution to their economic troubles was being resolved by printing more money, alarm bells went off. This signaled to the international community that Germany did not have enough money to pay for even the most basic of needs. Foreign investors quickly removed their money, and the economy sank further into a quagmire.

Piling onto the problem, the strike had caused the price of goods to soar even higher. Prices rose so rapidly that goods that had been marginally affordable earlier in a day were unattainable by the end of it. To help remedy this, striking workers were being paid twice a day. Each time they were paid, they were allowed time to go shop in order to buy necessities before prices rose any further.

German journalist Egon Larsen described this scene, which was played out around the country daily. He said, "As soon as the factory gates opened and the workers streamed out, pay packets (often in old cigar boxes) in their hands, a kind of relay race began: the wives grabbed the money, rushed to the nearest shops, and bought food before prices went up again. Salaries always lagged behind, the employees on monthly pay were worse off than workers on weekly. People living on fixed incomes sank into deeper and deeper poverty."

By the fall of 1923, those who wanted to buy a simple loaf of bread had to pay a shocking two hundred billion marks. People brought massive amounts of money to stores in backpacks, laundry baskets, and wheelbarrows. Sometimes thieves would approach those carrying their money and steal the basket or cart the money was being carried in, dumping out the currency notes and leaving them in the streets as worthless. Some used the paper notes to make kites for their kids, as they were useless.

One German writer illustrated how bad inflation had gotten through a telling of his own experience. "One fine day I dropped into a cafe to have a coffee. As I went in I noticed the price was 5000 marks—just about what I had in my pocket. I sat down, read my paper, drank my coffee, and spent altogether about one hour in the cafe, and then asked for the bill. The waiter duly presented me with a bill for 8000 marks. 'Why 8000 marks?' I asked. The mark had dropped in the meantime, I was told. So, I gave the waiter all the money I had, and he was generous enough to leave it at that." As a consequence of the high-speed inflation, many restaurants did not even bother placing prices on their menus anymore; they would change faster than people could eat their food.

Some small businesses began paying their workers in something they could actually use—foodstuffs. A system was worked out to parcel out food according to what each worker would be owed. Each payday, workers would line up to receive flour, fats, live poultry, and anything else their employer was able to buy in bulk.

Those who had retired and lived on a fixed income now found that their pensions had become worthless. These people quickly began to suffer poverty. By the time winter came, the poor were burning their furniture to keep from freezing to death.

The critical situation fostered ever-greater resentment toward the government and brought up questions that it could not find satisfactory answers for. And so, blame would need to be cast somewhere, or else the people would look elsewhere for solutions. One of these was the National Socialist German Workers' Party.

Chapter 9 – Assassination of Character

"How did big business win? Well, from the very beginning they figured their prices in gold value, selling their goods at gold value prices and paying their workers in inflated marks."—Ema von Pustau, Hamburg citizen, 1920s

As was obvious, the economic crisis profoundly affected the German society as a whole. But small business owners, workers, and others became increasingly angry as they saw one group that remained untouched amidst the hyperinflation fallout—wealthy landowners and large industrialists. While the middle class was losing everything, big business was actually prospering.

Ema von Pustau, quoted above, expressed what many were feeling during that time when she said, "We were deceived, too. We used to say, 'All of Germany is suffering from inflation.' It was not true. There is no game in the whole world in which everyone loses. Someone has to be the winner. The winners in our inflation were big business men in the cities and the Green Front, from peasants to the Junkers, in the country. The great losers were the working class and above all the middle class, who had most to lose."

Those living near the border of Switzerland saw a regular influx of tourists ready to spend. As they easily shelled out money, shopping for luxury goods, eating at cafes, and flocking to glamourous locales, disgruntled Germans took notice. Envy over the visitors' ability to afford things of which they could not even dream quickly turned to contempt. That contempt turned into a great deal of anti-foreign sentiment and polarized nationalistic feelings among the people.

It wasn't just against foreigners, the government, and big business the people hated. Another group began to feel the loathing of the people: the Jewish population. Rumors began to spread around the country, and even those who previously had not harbored any anti-Semitic feelings began to wonder if the poor economic situation had something to do with the Jews within the country.

It was unlikely that those rumors and the feelings that accompanied them were spread unintentionally. Around the country, small groups full of disaffected nationalists and former soldiers had cropped up. One of the most prominent of these was the National Socialist German Workers' Party, headed by a far-right radical, a man named Adolf Hitler. He and his Workers' Party advocated for a strong, unified central state made up of people of the "master race." Other inferior races, particularly the Jews, were the main target of their hatred. Hitler's charismatic and impassioned speeches caused people to take notice, and his words stuck within their ears, even as they went on their own way.

Anti-Jewish sentiments had really started to take hold the year before, in 1919. Many believed that rich Jews were controlling the economy and prospering while other Germans suffered miserably. In particular, their rage came to be focused on Walter Rathenau, the unabashedly Jewish foreign minister of the Weimar Republic.

Rathenau was an industrialist with great business and financial acumen, and he used his engineering and electronics conglomerate to almost single-handedly keep the German economy afloat during the Great War. But instead of being a savior of the national economy, many warily looked at him as its overlord. Anti-Semitic nationalists looked past his financial genius and saw only a Jew who wanted to corner the markets for himself and his people.

When the newly born republic asked Rathenau to become the foreign minister, even his own mother panicked, knowing the target on him would grow ever larger. He not only insisted that the country honor the terms of the hated Treaty of Versailles but also added fuel to the right wing's burning rage when he negotiated the Treaty of Rapallo. Though the treaty was pragmatic, militarily strategic, and, he had hoped, economically advantageous, his enemies chose to ignore these facts. Instead, all they saw was a German Jew making shady deals with Russian Jews who held political ideologies to which they were opposed.

Rathenau's actions were virtually treasonous in their eyes. Opposers marched through the streets, spewing hatred with such words as, "Knallt ab den Walther Rathenau! Der Gott-verfluchte Juden-sau!" (Translation: "Knock down Walther Rathenau! The God-forsaken Jewish sow!")

The hatred they expressed in words eventually turned into tragic action. Underground terrorist group Organisation Consul, believing the forged and now debunked Protocols of the Elders of Zion propaganda, set their sights on Rathenau as a member of the Jewish conclave secretly plotting world domination.

On June 24th, 1922, two ex-military officers, along with a young driver, ambushed Rathenau as he rode in his chauffeur-driven limousine. After spraying the car with bullets, a number of which struck the minister, the assassins threw a grenade into the vehicle to ensure they finished the job. Rathenau sustained catastrophic injuries, with his jaw and spine being shattered. He died within minutes of the attack.

The killers were not hailed as heroes for their deed. There was widespread public revulsion over the murder, as the people condemned the act.

Unfortunately, that kind of bigoted vitriol did not stay contained to those within radical political parties and groups. WWI veteran Henry Buxbaum spoke about an experience he had aboard a train, one that highlighted how the poor opinion of Jews was taking hold among the German people. Describing what he heard, he recounted,

"The train was pitch-dark. The lights were out, nothing uncommon after the war when the German railroads were in utter disrepair and very few things functioned orderly...That night, we were seven or eight people in the dark, fourth-class compartment, sitting in utter silence till one of the men started the usual refrain: 'Those [...] Jews, they are at the root of all our troubles.' Quickly, some of the others joined in. I couldn't see them and had no idea who they were, but from their voices they sounded like younger men. They sang the same litany over and over again, blaming the Jews for everything that had gone wrong with Germany and for anything else wrong in this world. It went on and on, a cacophony of obscenities, becoming more and more vicious and at the same time more unbearable with each new sentence echoing in my ears."

With the economic situation in the country at a tipping point and citizens being fed up with the terrible suffering it had brought on, it was no surprise when rioting erupted in Berlin. On November 5th and 6th, 1923, a mob thirty thousand strong brought their protest to Berlin. The country could not continue as it was, and the people would not stop shouting until change was affected.

Yet as much as they blamed the government, many of those protesting were also placing the blame for this plight on the Jews. Conspiracies were flying that the Jews were not only in control of the German economy but that they were also in an international plot bent on world domination.

Although false information was being spread about the country's economy and who should take the blame, one thing remained true—a dramatic change was needed. Bold reform was on the horizon.

Chapter 10 – The 102-Day Chancellorship and the Dawes Plan

When Gustav Stresemann became chancellor on August 12th, 1923, Weimar was deep into its moment of crisis. Fortunately for the republic, Stresemann showed up ready to work. As the founder of the German People's Party and, previous to the war, a staunch monarchist, he formed a coalition with the SPD, DDP (German Democratic Party), and Centre Party.

Stresemann was an academic intellectual with a head for business. It was just what the Weimar economy would need: someone with the financial acumen to pull the economy from the abyss. It was the moment of crisis he seemed born for.

The newly appointed chancellor didn't just understand finances; he also understood diplomacy and politics and how he could work them to his advantage. And just what did the Allied countries and other nations want from Germany the most? Compliance with the Treaty of Versailles. It didn't matter how much Germany hated the terms; they had already been agreed to in the interest of peace. And Stresemann knew that making great efforts to comply with the terms (unlike other governmental figures who had sought to circumvent or completely ignore them) would improve the country's international relationships. If the international community was happy with Weimar's genuine attempts to comply, Stresemann would stand a chance of securing reasonable treaty revisions in his favor.

But first, he had to use the controversial Article 48, one that his predecessor Ebert had employed 136 times during his tenure in office. On September 26th, 1923, Stresemann would use it to declare a state of emergency while suspending seven other articles of the constitution.

The steps that followed were wildly unpopular. He insisted that the republic resume paying reparations—an order that appeared counterintuitive as well as impossible in the midst of hyperinflationary chaos.

Next, he called off the passive resistance of the workers in the Ruhr region and ordered them to go back to their jobs. It was in direct conflict with the previous administration's strategy but one that was necessary to reset the wheels of the economy back into motion. It was the only common-sense move to be made.

Once those steps were put into place, Stresemann set to work on stabilizing the nation's currency. The value of the mark had fallen so low that by the fall of 1923, farmers refused to take it in exchange for produce. In fact, that year, they harvested crops but let them rot in their warehouses rather than sell them for worthless marks. Meanwhile, grocery store shelves remained empty, and people in the cities starved. This state of affairs could not continue.

Stresemann put the matter in the hands of Finance Minister Hans Luther and Managing Director of the Darmstadt and National Bank, Hjalmar Schacht. Schacht worked tirelessly, making phone call after phone call to anyone who might be able to help, including the Americans. The men strategized on how to renegotiate and restructure the country's debts.

On October 15th, their hard work paid off, and a new currency was born to the republic—the Rentenmark. Backed by mortgaging all the real property in Germany and issuing bonds against the nation's industries, the Rentenmark replaced the previous German Papiermark. The value ratio of Papiermarks to Rentenmarks was one trillion to one.

After the incredible success Stresemann had in bringing the Weimar economy back under control, he and his cabinet resigned on November 23rd, 1923, after only 102 days in office. However, Stresemann's work was not finished.

Stresemann's successor, Wilhelm Marx, saw his value and immediately appointed him minister of foreign affairs. Stresemann got right back to work. His first order of business as foreign minister was accepting the American-proposed Dawes Plan.

When reparation payments from Germany had dried up, Europe's powers could not agree on what to do about it. So, the Allied Reparations Committee called on Chicago banker (and former Budget Bureau director) Charles Dawes to look into the issue.

Together, Stresemann and Dawes began to work out a plan that they hoped all parties could live with. In April 1924, their proposal was presented to the committee. The crux of the proposal was that Germany's reparation obligations would be restructured and reasonably based on its ability to pay. For the time being, Germany's annual payment schedule would be reduced, but it would slowly increase as its economy recovered. The full amount due was still in question, and the plan left that to be determined later on.

Under the new plan, federal economic policy-making would be internationally supervised to ensure Germany maintained control of the situation. In return, foreign banks would give the Weimar government $200 million in US market-backed loans.

As much as the Dawes Plan benefited the Weimar government, it also benefited the United States and other Allied countries. While France and Great Britain received their much sought-after reparation payments, they were then, in turn, able to use the money to pay back their war debts to the United States. The plan was a win all around.

Stresemann's decisive actions, along with the Dawes Plan, worked to stabilized Weimar Germany. Over the next few years, foreign investments would be made in the recovering republic, returning gold to its treasury and allowing the economy to regain strength.

But as Stresemann had been working feverishly to stabilize the country's financial situation, he also had other metaphorical fires to put out, namely, a coup.

Chapter 11 – The Beer Hall Putsch

The stormtroopers had gathered in the dark in the Bürgerbräukeller beer hall. Inside, average citizens, businessmen, Munich's police chief and some of his deputies, and leaders of the Bavarian government were listening to a political speech. They had no idea that they were targets of an extremist political group.

A half-hour earlier, a political party leader, whom the police recognized as someone invited to the talks, went to speak to the police guarding the hall on the streets. There were too many citizens milling about the outside of the hall, he told them. They should clear the streets. The police took his suggestion and did just as he said. Little did they know they were clearing the way for the trucks his troops would soon arrive in.

At 8:30 p.m. on November 8th, 1923, troop commander Hermann Göring, a decorated WWI fighter pilot, gave the order to storm the hall. As stormtroopers burst into the hall, those inside were immediately thrust into a panic.

The National German Socialist Workers' Party leader, Adolf Hitler, waited in the antechamber to make his entrance. A high school dropout and failed artist, Hitler was injured by mustard gas during his

WWI military service. Later, as a police spy in Munich, he infiltrated the small German Workers' Party. Hitler was opposed to the despised treaty and what it stood for, as well as being disenchanted with the economic condition of the country. He expressed a desire to "save Germany." The German Workers' Party, with its nationalistic and anti-Semitic policies, was a perfect fit for his ideologies.

In 1919, he actually joined the party and soon became one of its leaders. His charismatic speeches in beer halls over the next few years garnered some attention, and by 1921, he was the leader of the National German Socialist Workers' Party, better known as the Nazi Party. Inspired by Benito Mussolini's "March on Rome," which took place in the previous October, he planned his own "March on Berlin." This "march" was to be a complete national government takeover.

Now, in his dramatic entrance, Hitler walked into the main hall, and throwing his half-liter beer glass, he grabbed his pistol and aimed at the ceiling, firing off a shot. The panicked crowd was stunned, and through the din of confusion, he shouted, "Silence!" The crowd immediately quieted.

The dramatic effect of his entrance soon began to diminish, as he had to elbow and fight his way through the crowd to reach the podium as more stormtroopers poured in the doors behind him. A police major tried to stop his progress, but Hitler pointed a pistol at him, and the major backed down.

Some in the crowd tried to escape only to be turned back. Those who persisted in trying to leave were punched and kicked by troopers. Alarm set in as exits were blocked and machine guns were set up near the doors. State Commissioner Gustav von Kahr, who had been giving the speech, stared in confusion as Hitler approached him at the podium. He noted that Kahr appeared frightened and took a moment to ridicule the commissioner for his fear, especially since the hall was filled with Kahr's followers. Given the circumstances, it was a wholly unfair condemnation.

Yet Kahr yielded the podium, allowing Hitler to speak. A startling announcement followed.

"The National Revolution has begun!" Hitler shouted. "This building is occupied by 600 heavily armed men. No one may leave the hall. Unless there is immediate quiet I shall have a machine gun posted in the gallery. The Bavarian and Reich governments have been removed and a provisional national government formed. The barracks of the Reichswehr and police are occupied. The Army and the police are marching on the city under the swastika banner!"

The announcement was pure fabrication, a calculated bluff. The audience had no idea that it was not true, but one thing they did know was that the pistol Hitler waved wildly and the machine guns at the back were very real.

Afterward, Hitler, with the help of stormtroopers, brought Kahr, General Otto von Lossow, and Bavarian State Police Chief Hans Ritter von Seisser (known collectively as "the triumvirate," they were the three highest officials in Bavaria) into a side room. Pointing his revolver, Hitler told them, "No one leaves the room alive without my permission."

Hitler then demanded that the men join his revolution, and in turn, they would be given key positions in the new government. Although the men had been calling for change, this was not what they had in mind. The men glared at Hitler in silence.

Becoming agitated, Hitler waved his pistol and told the men, "I have four shots in my pistol! Three for my collaborators if they abandon me. The last bullet for myself!" Then putting the gun to his own head, he told them, "If I am not victorious by tomorrow afternoon, I shall be a dead man!"

Kahr was unintimidated. He told Hitler, "You can have me shot or shoot me yourself. Whether I die or not is no matter." Von Lossow remained stubbornly silent.

Von Seisser had only reproach for Hitler, condemning him for breaking his promise to not make a putsch against the police. Hitler did not deny this but instead told Seisser, "Forgive me, but I had to for the sake of the Fatherland."

Outside in the hall, resentment was growing. One of the businessmen shouted at the police, "Don't be cowards as in 1918. Shoot!" But the police were not inclined to comply. The Nazis had a spy within the police, Wilhelm Frick. Beforehand, he had already warned police at the beer hall not to interfere.

The crowd continued to grow unhappier with this turn of events. Göring felt that he needed to step in to ensure the situation remained calm. Going to the podium, he addressed the crowd, telling them, "You have nothing to fear. We have the friendliest intentions. For that matter, you've got no cause to grumble. You've got beer!"

Fifteen minutes had passed with the triumvirate in the side room. And still, Hitler had not convinced the men to join him, even at the end of a pistol. He would not wait any longer. Rushing into the hall, Hitler addressed the crowd, informing them with a shout, "The Bavarian Ministry is removed! The government of the November Criminals and the Reich president are declared to be removed! A new national government will be named this very day here in Munich...The task of the provisional German National Government is to organize a march to that sinful Babel, Berlin, and save the German people...Tomorrow you will find either a National Government in Germany or us dead!"

The change that came over the crowd was almost instantaneous. Hitler's words had their effect, and they were greeted with loud cheers and wild applause. Little did they know that not one word of it was true. Encouraged and emboldened by the crowd's reaction, Hitler continued the falsehood. With emotion in his voice, he told the crowds that Kahr, Lossow, and Seisser were still struggling to make a decision. He asked the crowd, "May I say to them that you will stand behind them?" The crowds shouted their affirmative consent. Over the din, Hitler cried passionately, "Either the German revolution begins tonight, or we will all be dead by dawn!"

Hitler returned to the locked side room. There, WWI hero General Erich Ludendorff, who Hitler had just named head of the national army, stood before the triumvirate in the full military uniform of an imperial officer. He entreated and advised the triumvirate that they should cooperate, especially since the crowd was behind them. Ludendorff's speech had its effect, and the men reluctantly agreed. But their agreement would eventually prove to be a ruse.

Everyone in the side room marched back out to the podium, where each member of the triumvirate gave a brief speech. Their words were met with thunderous applause. Hitler, giddy with happiness that his plan was back on track, took the podium to speak the final words of the meeting. He told the crowd that he wanted to fulfill a promise he had made to himself while in the military as he lay blind and crippled five years before. That promise? He would not rest until "the November criminals were overthrown" and "a Germany of power and greatness, of freedom and splendor" arose "on the ruins of the wretched Germany of today." The crowds roared their approval and broke out in patriotic song. Hitler basked in the euphoria of the moment.

As the joyous crowd departed, Bavarian cabinet members, including the triumvirate, were detained. Hitler received word of clashes between two military units and left to investigate the matter personally, leaving Ludendorff in charge. That seemingly inconsequential decision would be Hitler's first fatal mistake.

Von Lossow was the first of the triumvirate to make a move. He told Ludendorff that he needed to get to his office at army headquarters so he could give orders in connection with the new government. When some in the room objected to letting him leave, Ludendorff replied, "I forbid you to doubt the word of a German officer." Once von Lossow left, Kahr and von Seisser took their cue and slipped away, disappearing into the night.

After Hitler failed to secure the surrender of the soldiers holed up in the army barracks, he returned to the beer hall. His previous euphoria quickly vanished. Having expected to see the triumvirate and others busily working on plans for the Berlin march and other tasks necessary to take over Munich, he was shocked to see that they were gone and that no progress had been made in moving on with his plan. He was further deflated to find out that though stormtroopers had taken over one of the army barracks in the city, the revolutionary forces had otherwise remained essentially idle.

Most troopers in the city acted less like revolutionaries and more like bands of thugs, doing little more than harassing Jews and taking custody of a few political opponents. Meanwhile, policemen around the city scrambled to get back to police headquarters. But in a ludicrous turn of events, the only transportation available to them was the tram. Officers piled in and made their way through the streets, putschists obliviously marching right past them.

Later that night, a few feeble attempts were made to capture strategic locations. Though some succeeded, many failed. One of those failures was the attempted takeover of a police station. Former Munich police chief turned Hitler supporter went along with stormtroopers and an army officer to take the station. Upon arriving, the entire group was promptly arrested. However, another band did have somewhat more success trying to take over a different police station.

Military commander Ernst Röhm and a group of his stormtroopers descended upon the Wehrkreis headquarters and forced the surrender of the officers with some difficulty. Shortly afterward, Major Schwandner arrived at the headquarters, having heard about the putsch. Police Captain Daser immediately informed him that he found the whole situation fishy, unsure whether to trust Röhm even after he told them that the takeover was being done with the approval of Kahr, von Lossow, and von Seisser.

When Röhm's personal friend and political opponent Major Karl von Loeffelholz arrived at the headquarters to find out what was happening, Röhm had him arrested and kept him tucked away in his office. When Röhm left the room, Loeffelholz quickly changed into civilian clothes. Leaving the office, he walked right out the door of the station without any problems. He went straight to von Lossow to report what was happening.

Other than this, virtually no other key areas of the city were taken over by Hitler's supporters, not even the telegraph office. Here was another critical tactical error. By failing to secure the telegraph office, news of the coup was allowed to reach Berlin. The army commander in Berlin replied, ordering the Bavarian army to suppress the putsch. Though a few junior officers defected to Hitler, the bulk of the Munich military units were ready to carry out the orders from Berlin. They were particularly bitter that Hitler had dared threaten General von Lossow with a gun, a breach of etiquette that would usually call for the offender to be pistol-whipped with an officer's sidearm.

Von Lossow, now free, coordinated with General Jakob Ritter von Danner to send messages to outlying garrisons, calling on them to rush into the city with reinforcements. Meanwhile, Hitler desperately searched for the triumvirate, sending messengers around the city to try and make contact with them.

But the next morning, Kahr was already in action. Recovering his courage, he knew the best way to remain free from Hitler's grasp was to remove himself and the government to Regensburg. But before he left, he made sure that the whole city knew where he stood. He had placards made and posted around the city condemning "the scene of disgusting violence" perpetrated by Hitler and his ilk. He also informed the city that he, von Seisser, and von Lossow had only agreed to Hitler's terms under duress and that they could now consider the declarations they made null and void. And finally, he announced that he was dissolving the German Workers' Party and its military units.

Hitler saw his revolution rapidly unraveling. He firmly believed that a revolution could only be successful if the existing institutions, such as the police, army, and other political entities, supported it. He now had virtually none of that. Groping for a solution, he proposed to Ludendorff that they go to the countryside and rally the peasants to their cause. Ludendorff quickly squashed the idea.

Hitler became so desperate to make things work that he even appealed to Bavarian Crown Prince Rupprecht to make Kahr, von Seisser, and von Lossow peaceably honor their words. The trouble was, Rupprecht had roundly condemned the revolt and called for its suppression, not to mention the fact that he was bitter enemies with Ludendorff. The former royal did not even deign to reply.

The tide continued to turn for the worse. Hitler and Ludendorff were on the cusp of a civil war with the national army. This was not at all how they had pictured events would unfold. They had planned to create a revolution with the army, not against it. As much as Hitler's speeches had called for violence, he was reluctant to spill the blood of those who hated the republic as he did. Ludendorff, although having told his wife that he would string the president and his men from nooses and "gladly watch them dangle from the gallows," did not want to commit acts of violence against fellow soldiers or the police (many of whom were ex-soldiers).

Still, Ludendorff came up with a plan for how they might avoid bloodshed but still come out victorious. And it was a bold plan indeed. Certain that soldiers and police, who revered him as a legendary commander and war hero, would not dare fire upon him, he proposed to Hitler that they take their followers and simply march into the middle of the city and take over the government buildings. He believed that once there, the police would not only leave him undisturbed but also join him in the fight.

Hitler had his doubts about Ludendorff's claims, but the veteran general was highly confident, and there were no other possibilities for regaining control. So, on the morning of November 9th, Hitler,

Ludendorff, and three thousand armed men began marching on Munich, their swastika banner unfurled before them. Having secured a couple of cabinet members to use as hostages the night before, the column faced little resistance. In just over an hour, they reached the War Ministry building. There, they faced an obstacle that they had not expected.

They had come face to face with their fellow soldiers who surrounded the Reichswehr, with only some thin pieces of barbed wire standing between them. As the soldiers on both sides stood staring at each other, no one had the heart to fire a single shot. Wanting to keep his men progressing, Ludendorff led them through a narrow passage. Coming out near a spacious plaza, the troops were met by policemen one hundred strong. Even though the police were greatly outnumbered, they courageously refused to back down when Hitler ordered their surrender.

A single shot rang out. Immediately, a volley of shots erupted from both sides. The gun battle lasted a mere sixty seconds, but as the last shot reverberated and the chaos stopped, the street was littered with bodies of the dead and injured. Among them lay two of Hitler's key men, while he himself also clutched the pavement in pain from a dislocated shoulder. Ludendorff was nowhere to be seen.

But the legendary soldier had not slinked away in cowardice. When others had dived for the ground, Ludendorff and his adjutant, Major Streck, stood tall. Facing down the police muzzles, they marched straight between them and into the plaza. He and the major stood alone in the Odeonsplatz; not one Nazi had followed them, not even Hitler himself.

Ludendorff was arrested where he stood. That moment, when he realized no soldiers marched behind him, was agonizingly bitter for the general. He swore from that time on, he would never recognize another German soldier, nor would he ever wear a uniform again.

As for Hitler's other henchmen, they fared little better. Göring, who was injured by bullets, was in an ironic twist of fate; he was given first aid by a Jewish bank proprietor who had been nearby. He was thereafter smuggled into Austria, where he was admitted to the hospital. Rudolf Hess, a leading member of the Nazi Party, also ran for Austria. The two managed to escape arrest.

Röhm, however, was arrested right there at the War Ministry. Within a few days, he was joined in prison by the other rebel leaders. As soon as the guns had stopped firing, Hitler was the first to get to his feet and run in retreat. He fled to a waiting car, where he was whisked away to the country home of friends. He hid in their attic for two days, despondent and threatening to commit suicide. He, too, was arrested a couple of days later.

By all appearances, Hitler's feeble attempt at a revolution spelled doom for his political career. Hitler, on the other hand, brightened with hope when he found out he would have a public trial. He knew that the press would be at the courthouse reporting it all and that his name would be plastered in headlines across the country, giving him the notoriety he sought.

Many of the judges during this period were lenient toward right-wing extremists, as they were sympathetic toward their claims of acting from sincere and patriotic motives. The judge in this case was no different. Still, Hitler put on his best show for the trial. He went into court with his Iron Cross proudly pinned to his chest and displayed for all to see. When given the chance to speak in court, he used it to continue spreading the propaganda he had been spouting in beer halls. He persisted in claiming what many were already inclined to believe—that the national government had betrayed Germany and its people when they signed the Treaty of Versailles. Hitler showed no remorse for his actions, only justification, insinuating that he acted to stop the "clear and imminent communist threat to Germany."

Even though he was convicted, he was sentenced to a mere five years in prison for high treason, , the minimum sentence allowed by law. Despite the conviction and criticism from left- and right-wing newspapers alike, Hitler knew this would not be the end for him. Despite the botched putsch, the event turned Hitler from traitor to national hero and patriot in the eyes of many.

Chapter 12 – The Renaissance and the "Babylon of the 1920s"

With the economy getting back on its feet and the political situation somewhat stabilized, the republic was well on its way to recovery by the end of 1924. The country entered its golden era, which some would call the "Weimar Renaissance."

Stresemann, now acting as foreign minister, next focused on what he considered one of the most important objectives of the government, "removing the strangler from our throat," as he put it to former Crown Prince Wilhelm. That "strangler" was the French-Belgian occupation of the Ruhr.

Stresemann took the initiative to reach out for a peaceful solution, sending a note to the Allies in February 1925 stating his desire for rapprochement. Between October 5th and 16th, 1925, Stresemann and Allied dignitaries met in Switzerland to discuss the terms of the withdrawal. The Locarno Pact was drawn up, with France and Belgium agreeing to settle the terms of the treaty with Germany in a peaceful manner. Each country also agreed to not invade each other's borders nor resort to war, attack, or invasion but to strive to settle matters through peaceful diplomacy.

Stresemann's strategy to improve relations with the other countries succeeded brilliantly. France and Belgium withdrew their forces from Germany, and tensions between the countries died down. Germany's international relationships improved so much that the next year, the country was accepted into the League of Nations.

On the home front, people saw an improvement in their day-to-day living conditions. There was now money in the government coffers to build new public institutions like schools and hospitals. Though unemployment still remained an issue, those who had jobs saw working conditions improve—their wages were increasing and working hours decreasing. Worker morale started to rise.

Though unemployment remained high, the morale of the country began to rise. And with this rise in morale, there was a shift in focus, as the people finally felt relief from their economic and political woes. Culture in Germany was now able to flourish. This new era lent itself to fresh ideas, allowing art and architectural ideas to progress. Weimar forevermore became synonymous with modernism.

Avant-garde artists formed themselves into a loose artist conclave called the November Group. The group, which started in 1918, began to grow to include about one hundred artists from different genres. Painters, sculptors, music composers, filmmakers, playwrights, architects, and others projected a spirit of radicalism through their works.

In particular, the Bauhaus style (also known as International style), named for the famed design and architecture school, took center stage. In an experiment in modernism, the style promoted the harmony between function and design, with a heavy focus on geometric shapes and patterns. The style began to appear everywhere, including new interior and exterior architecture, furniture, and décor.

Ultra-modern and experimental forms of art appeared around the country. For example, Dada artist Max Ernst had an ax placed near his exhibition pieces "for the convenience of anyone who wanted to attack the work." Dadaist Kurt Schwitters filled the rooms of a two-story house with sculptures he made using found and ephemeral objects. New Objectivity artists cast aside rules and the more traditional and idealistic Expressionism art form that focused on elements like fantasy, romanticism, and emotion. New Objectivity focused on subjects that were factual (such as the harsh reality of war) and created realistic works through the use of precision and deliberateness.

Other genres of art, such as literature and cinema, also dealt with subjects such as politics and the failure of it, as well as the failures of society, protest, and propaganda. Films used exaggerated acting techniques, unrealistic sets, and darker storylines in the Expressionist style. The war and the years that followed it had a deep impact on the German people, and this became obvious in the numerous expressions made through art forms that proliferated during the Weimar era.

But not all art forms that became popular dealt with dark themes or hard realities. American jazz, with its cacophony of atonal and often uplifting beats, became wildly popular. Many classical composers, even in the midst of a modern classical boom, became enamored with jazz and drifted over to the genre.

Berlin not only grew into the intellectual and artistic center of the country but also of Europe. It established itself as a true cosmopolitan city. Besides pioneering modernist works of literature, theater, and art, it also nurtured ground-breaking works and ideas in scientific fields like sociology, psychoanalysis, math, and physics. Some of the century's (and history's) greatest minds, like physicists Max Planck and Albert Einstein, were hard at work during this period. Many intellectuals formed themselves into a thinkers' group called the Berlin Circle.

But aside from art and intellectualism, Berlin underwent a different kind of cultural revolution as well. With censorship all but done away with, it earned a reputation for decadence. Creative freedoms and free expression of thought abounded. It allowed more conventional, or what some might consider austere, social norms to loosen their grip. Anything seemed to go, or as one person put it, "you could find almost anything there, and maybe everything."

If one had money, one had access to just about anything. Illicit drugs flowed freely, nights were spent in hedonistic partying, and sexual freedoms were explored. Aside from traditional theater, those looking for something risqué could drop in for a few drinks and a provocative cabaret show. Pop culture icons like Marlene Dietrich appeared; she became well known for her film portrayals of "loose" women. Other women, like actress and dancer Anita Berber, became notorious for their erotic dance performances at nighttime venues around the city. The line between underground culture and what was considered acceptable and legitimate performance suddenly became blurred. These lightning-quick shifts in culture earned Berlin the nickname the "Babylon of the 1920s."

Berlin's cultural revolution was in many ways a coping mechanism for people who were dealing with the aftermath of the war and economic depression. But there were also those who had to deal with the war's aftermath in ways that were not as "fun." Many remained jobless and resorted to petty crimes, often out of necessity. Among Berlin's unsavory underworld could be found prostitutes, drug dealers, black marketeers, and organized crime gangsters. Although these things still remained illegal, the demand for the illicit increased, and those who participated now operated somewhat more freely in this new liberal age.

In many ways, the country had indeed made progress and taken some huge leaps forward during this short, golden five-year period. However, the prosperity and the good times they were experiencing were about to come to a crashing halt.

Chapter 13 – The Great Depression

With its golden age in full swing and economic health in recovery, things were looking up for the Weimar Republic. And now, in 1929, a new economic plan, one that would complement the Dawes Plan, was proposed to further help the country back onto its feet financially.

Owen Young, who was appointed by the Allied Reparations Committee, was tasked with restructuring Germany's war debt. The Young Plan, which was proposed in June 1929, would further reduce Germany's reparation bill to a mere eight billion dollars to be paid in annual increments over the next fifty-nine years. But if Germany didn't have the $473 million for an annual payment, they could pay just one-third, and it would be considered satisfactory.

A still-bitter Britain balked at the terms, but the heavily involved American presence in the plan-making, including one of the world's most prominent bankers, J. P. Morgan, saw benefits to it. Allowing Germany to grow as an economic resource had its plus side. They didn't care if the European allies viewed them as being "too soft" on Germany.

The plan would allow Germany to become a valuable business trading partner to the US. But besides economic benefits, the US was banking on it having a political benefit as well. They believed that if the Germans could embrace their capitalist ideology, they would not turn to the "plague from the east," Russian communism, that constantly threatened to rise up.

But as much as America was aiding Germany, it was about to face its own terrifying economic crisis. It was a crisis that would have a ripple effect around the world, including Weimar. And it would doom the newly formulated Young Plan as well.

The United States was struggling with its own postwar problems. Unemployment had gone up, and wages had gone down. US banks held enormous unliquidated loans, as people took out large personal debts with exorbitantly high-interest rates.

With economic problems rife, many Americans took to investing in the loosely regulated Wall Street stock market, hoping to earn their fortune. In early 1929, an influx of investments created artificial stock values. Company market values grew higher than their actual value. By early September, stock prices peaked at an all-time high.

It did not take long for prices to begin dropping, triggering panic and mass sell-offs. In just one month, market values had been halved. On October 24th, 1929, a day that became known as "Black Thursday," the American Wall Street stock market fell in a devastating crash. Like a boulder dropped into a calm pond, the ripple effects could not be contained. The sudden and intense economic ripples from the crash quickly reached Germany.

Germany had been reliant on a flow of money from American banks to remain stable. But with the ripples spreading out into the interconnected international business network, there was almost no stable economy to be found in the entire world. Cash from the US to Germany dried up, and Americans scrambled to resolve their own issues. The US was far from being able to lend money, as it was urgently calling for repayment of their own international loans. The

US had to stop buying German industrial goods, putting a moratorium on foreign imports.

Germany now tumbled back into an economic crisis. And the effects were devastating. It could not endure the end of US financial support. No longer able to rely on US exports, factories dramatically downsized or closed altogether. Unemployment again began to rise quickly. By the end of the year, 1.5 million Germans were out of work, more than double the previous year.

During the golden years, millions of German factory workers prospered—they were the most well-paid blue-collar workers in all of Europe during those years. And now they found themselves out of work and with no way to productively spend their time.

Christopher Isherwood, a British novelist living in Berlin during the worst of the crisis, described the scenes of the unemployed that played out around the "damp, dreary town." Out-of-work young men went day after day being idle—hanging out around public washrooms, gossiping, playing checkers, lounging, or sharing racing tips and cigarette stumps plucked from the gutters. Some got creative and attempted to contrive work for themselves; they sold boot laces, opened car doors for people, and helped move crates in the market. Others turned to less than savory means of making money, like stealing and begging. The crash had taken an economic toll, and it also affected morale and the people's morals as well.

This time, unemployment did not just affect factory and other blue-collar workers. White-collar and professional jobs took a downturn, leaving many in the upper and middle classes out of work. University students, who had hoped their education would help them find employment, had nothing to turn to when they graduated. Sixty percent graduated only to be immediately unable to work.

Though there were some food shortages, a lack of food was not the problem for most. Having the means to obtain it was the greater issue. With no money for food, millions went hungry. Children fared the worst, with thousands dying from malnutrition and disease stemming from insufficient food and nutrients.

When Heinrich Brüning became chancellor in March 1930, he immediately had some tough decisions to make. In order to stimulate the economy, there would normally be a jump in government spending, which would thereby create jobs. However, Brüning greatly feared a repeat of the hyperinflation of the early 1920s and felt unemployment was the lesser evil in this situation. So, instead of spending, he looked for a way to increase cash flow to the government. In a controversial and often maligned move, he cut government spending and increased taxes on a population that was already heavily suffering.

Further worsening the situation, he mandated that wages and unemployment pay be cut in a misguided effort to lower prices and prevent inflation from getting out of control. He also wanted to put restrictions on business, finance, and social services. When parliament vehemently opposed these moves, surely the words of Freikorps founder General Kurt von Schleicher were ringing in Brüning's ears. He believed that the chancellor and president needed to govern with a strong hand, claiming that was what the people wanted. He saw the numerous political parties of the Reichstag as a hindrance to effectively solving any issues, especially because each party was focused on its own interests, making it difficult to get a majority agreement on anything.

But it hardly mattered whether parliament agreed; Brüning had the backing of President Paul von Hindenburg. Using Article 48 of the constitution, he had Brüning's policies issued under the provision for national emergencies.

The measures were an utter failure. Unemployment actually increased, and the suffering of the people did as well. Those who had already lost their jobs sunk further into poverty. Bickering between political parties ramped up. Nazis and Communists began calling Brüning the "Hunger Chancellor."

Besides adding to the misery of the German people, the use of Article 48 at this time was another nail in the republic's coffin. It undermined the democratic process. In bypassing the Reichstag's objections, Brüning and von Hindenburg weakened its power and made democracy look like nothing but a façade.

It soon became apparent to Brüning that the republic was the most unpopular government that the country ever had. He desperately needed to find a viable solution to the country's plight. He could not rely on the political brilliance of Stresemann, who had died of a stroke in 1929. After a summer of pondering, he believed he had come up with the solution to reestablishing stability and prosperity. It was a tall order when the entire world was sinking further into the quagmire of the Great Depression.

Brüning would try to capitalize on the suspension of reparations payments that had been recently instituted by US President Herbert Hoover. Brüning would try to get the Allies to cancel the reparations altogether. If he could throw off this major millstone around the neck of the country, he believed that Germany would be able to emerge as an equal player among the big powers. He hoped it would restore confidence in democracy and take the wind out of political extremists' sails.

Brüning's plan worked this time. After negotiations, the European Allies at the Lausanne Conference of 1932 agreed to cancel Germany's reparation payment. Only the final payment would need to be made.

Although it was a success for Brüning, the cancellation of the reparations had little effect on the country or the economy. Germany had already stopped paying reparations since the beginning of the Great Depression, so the cancellation of the remaining payments did not do much to remedy the immediate situation.

Bankruptcy, hunger, malnutrition, and foreclosures continued to skyrocket. More and more people found themselves without homes to live in or food to feed themselves and their children. Men waded and foraged through garbage dumps, looking for the smallest scraps of food. Thousands stood in absurdly long lines, despairing as they waited their turn to try to get a job. Confidence in financial institutions plummeted, and thousands stood in line to withdraw money from the Berlin Post Office checkpoint. In turn, the banking system collapsed. The situation took a severe toll on the mental health of many, and suicides spiked.

Historian Irene Guenther noted that "anxiety and fear gripped the masses of unemployed men." That anxiety and fear manifested itself in another unexpected way—blatant gender prejudice against women with full-time jobs. Society pressured women to give up their jobs and go back to being housewives and mothers. Some happily returned to a traditional role in the home, but many women were disheartened. With the men out of work, many women needed their jobs for financial support. Others worried that it would be a permanent setback to the hard-won advances women had made over the years.

Aside from the economy and social issues, there was another tidal wave building, and it threatened to overtake the country. It was one that Brüning was even more desperate to stop.

Chapter 14 – The Downfall of Brüning

As the country again broiled with resentments, it sat on the brink of civil war. People were frightened and angry about their plight and the lack of effective solutions being issued by their democratic government.

Brüning sensed the tide turning, knowing that more and more of the discontented populace were turning toward extremist political parties like communism and fascism, which offered seemingly simple solutions to the complex problems facing the nation. By 1932, more than half of those who held seats in the Reichstag belonged to far-right- or far-left-wing political parties bent on destroying the Weimar Republic. But what alarmed Brüning the most was the growing support for the Nazi Party—support that allowed them to have a greater majority in the Reichstag.

Brüning worried about the upcoming elections. He knew that even if von Hindenburg was reelected, the elderly president was highly unlikely to live through his next seven-year term. He might live another year or two into his presidency, but if and when he died, the path to the presidency would be left wide open for Hitler. Brüning realized that he would need to take drastic action to prevent the Nazis from gaining power. He needed to cut them off at the knees. So, he formulated a bold plan—he would try to reinstitute the monarchy.

Knowing that he would not have widespread support, not even from President Hindenburg, Brüning needed to employ a more long-game strategy. If he could get parliament to simply extend Hindenburg's term, a possibility if he could get two-thirds of the vote from both houses of parliament, he would then present his proposal to restore the monarchy. Hindenburg would serve as president regent until his death, and then the crown prince would assume the throne.

The only problem was, Hindenburg was not on board. He would not dare to assume a role equivalent to that of the emperor he was forced to dismiss in 1918. Brüning tried to explain and reason with him. He told the aged president that the Social Democrats and workers' unions were behind the plan, if only because they, too, feared the Nazis' rise. He also told Hindenburg that his plan was less for an absolute monarchy and more for a constitutional or democratic one in the fashion of the British monarchy. This only served to enrage the president, who ordered Brüning to get out of his sight. Hindenburg would not support the monarchy plan, nor would he run for reelection.

Brüning felt forced to do the unthinkable. He would call on the Nazi Party to support his proposal for the continuance of Hindenburg's term. Hitler was called into a meeting with the chancellor and president. Still reeling from the recent suicide of his niece and lover Geli Raubal, Hitler went into the meeting lacking focus. But there was one thing that would not be in doubt by the end: Hitler's hatred for the republic.

When Brüning asked for Nazi Party's support for his plan, Hitler launched into a tirade against the republic. Unnerved by Hindenburg, Hitler had been hoping to impress the president with his rant, but he fell flat on his face. The president was undoubtedly not impressed, and he derisively called Hitler the "Bohemian corporal." Brüning, for his part, was deflated when it became apparent that he would get no support from this corner.

Schleicher, who had been Brüning's greatest supporter and the one who had propelled him to the chancellorship, was now soured on his successor. He saw him as a failure and disappointment. Not only had Brüning become the most unpopular chancellor the republic had seen, but he had also failed to keep his Centre Party in the majority or halt the Nazis' rise. Now, he bungled the plan to keep von Hindenburg in power. In his mind, Brüning needed to go. But for the moment, Schleicher had other schemes in the works that demanded his attention. The matter of Brüning would have to wait until after he could get Hindenburg's term extended.

Hitler, for his part, was regaining his confidence. When Brüning sent him a message calling him to another meeting in an effort to change his mind about the von Hindenburg plan, Hitler was ecstatic. But it wasn't because he had changed his mind or really cared about the matter. On receiving the telegram, he cried, "Now I have them in my pocket! They have recognized me as a partner in their negotiations!"

There was one important lesson that Hitler had learned from his failed Beer Hall Putsch. He knew his mistake had been a direct assault on the Weimar Republic. But now, he knew there was no way to destroy it without the support of the army and police. Brute force would not gain them to his side; it would only trigger a defensive response from the military.

Hitler knew that the only way he could take down this hated republic was from within. And to do that, he would use its own democratic ideals and processes against it. Instead of forcing the people to come to his side, he would use the freedoms democracy afforded him, namely the freedoms of speech and assembly. He would win over the people with his words. And with that, he would come to power through the popular vote.

With his second call to meet with the chancellor, Hitler saw the opportunity to get his foot in the door. Brüning, on the other hand, was playing with fire, a move that would ultimately help burn down the entire republic.

In January 1932, Hitler was vacillating on what was perhaps his most important decision to date. Would he run for president against Paul von Hindenburg, who had finally agreed to a bid for reelection? The elderly president seemed unbeatable. But once Hitler made the decision to run, he plowed ahead with the utmost confidence. After a long evening of planning between Hitler and German architect Albert Speer, one that included "a grandiose alteration of the national capital," Nazi insider Joseph Goebbels remarked that Hitler "speaks, acts and feels as if he is already in power."

There was only one problem with his plans for power—Hitler was not actually a citizen of Germany. Therefore, he was ineligible to run for president. Hitler hardly felt that this was an issue. After some creative political maneuvering, he was able to have himself made a citizen of Brunswick and thereby a citizen of Germany. He was then able to throw himself full force into his presidential campaign.

Brüning did everything in his power to support von Hindenburg, including reserving all radio time on government-controlled stations so that no other candidates (namely Hitler) would have the chance for their voice to be heard. Brüning's tactics infuriated Hitler.

Despite his utter confidence, Hitler found out that von Hindenburg was indeed unbeatable. Hitler lost both elections to the highly respected president by millions of votes. He did not even come close to beating von Hindenburg.

Disappointment did not render Hitler paralyzed. But before he could decide on his next move, he was dealt a hard blow by the Prussian police. The police raided the Nazi headquarters in Berlin and found evidence that a coup had been in the works. Documents showed that high-ranking Nazi leaders, with the assistance of the SA, were planning a forceful takeover of Germany if Hitler was elected president. Despite the fact that 400,000 SA had stationed themselves around Berlin and effectively closed off the city the night before the first election, Röhm (chief of the SA) played it off as a "precautionary" measure.

A deep uneasiness set in among government players. Goebbels wrote that "the word putsch haunts the air." Brüning and General Wilhelm Groener (now the minister of defense) feared civil war as much as they feared Hitler's rise in politics. They believed the solution to both these issues was to stamp out the SA.

In an April cabinet meeting, a proposal was set forth to immediately suppress the SA through a ban. Schleicher outwardly approved of the measure, but secretly, he was whispering objections into the president's ear. However, Hindenburg reluctantly agreed to sign the order. Nazi leadership was up in arms and talked about armed resistance. But Hitler knew he had to stick to his non-violent strategy. Besides, he had his eye on Schleicher, who he saw make an interesting move. Schleicher announced that he would resign his position. Though Goebbels astutely called his bluff a "maneuver," other political figures, including Hindenburg, Brüning, and Hitler himself, had not yet understood how crafty and treacherous General Schleicher really was. But they would find out soon enough.

Wanting to rid himself of Groener, Schleicher sought ways to undermine him in the eyes of the president. He then launched a slanderous smear campaign, spreading rumors that Groener was a Marxist, that he had turned to pacifism, that he was ill, and that his new baby had been conceived out of wedlock. All the while, Schleicher was conspiring with the SA.

In early May, Schleicher had a secret meeting with Hitler and men close to the president to discuss the final takedown of Groener and Brüning. That night, Goebbels reported, "Brüning will fall in a few days." But first, he would take care of Groener.

Two days after their meeting, Groener spoke in front of the Reichstag, defending the decision to ban the SA. Hermann Göring launched a vicious attack against the general. Groener, now all too aware of Schleicher's treachery, mounted a valiant defense of his position. But it was not enough. Nazi representatives hurled abuse after abuse at the defense minister, rendering him utterly exhausted and humiliated. As Groener tried to leave, Schleicher intercepted him in order to inform him in an icy manner that he "no longer enjoyed the confidence of the army and must resign." Groener refused to accept Schleicher at his word and appealed to the president whom he had served so well. However, Schleicher's campaign to shake Hindenburg's confidence in his loyal defense minister had worked. Hindenburg replied that he "regretted" it but that there was nothing he could do. Deeply bitter, Groener had no choice but to resign.

Groener's fall was a devastating loss to the country. He was the last officer left in the army who could lead capably and devotedly. There were none left like him. He was also the last man in the army standing between the republic and a SA reign of terror. His forced resignation left the government and, in particular, Brüning, alone and vulnerable to Schleicher and the Nazis.

Schleicher was delighted that things were going exactly according to plan. He now turned his attention to Brüning, who he wanted to see metaphorically hang. Schleicher had done what he could to undermine the chancellor in the eyes of the president, but in reality, he didn't have to do much. Brüning was coming close to hanging himself. Soon after Groener's downfall, Brüning tightened the noose around his own neck. His next move was the one that caused the death of his own career.

Brüning proposed that wealthy landowners in East Prussia sell the government their bankrupted estates. In turn, these could be given to poor, landless peasants. The other aristocrats in the region caught wind of this proposition and were outraged. They clamored for Brüning's resignation.

Schleicher and the Nazis knew Brüning's fate before he did and reveled in it. On May 19th, 1932, Brüning called Schleicher and reproached him for what he had done to Groener. But then, in a twist, he next asked Schleicher to replace Groener as the new defense minister. Schleicher's reply was chilling. "I will," he told Brüning, "but not in your government."

For Hindenburg, who had already cooled considerably toward the chancellor, the Prussia debacle was the last straw. On Sunday, May 29th, he called Brüning into his office and, without fanfare, abruptly demanded that he resign. Brüning complied the next day.

With Groener and Brüning gone, there was no one left to stem the growing tide of the Nazis, which was now swelling into a full-blown tidal wave with the help of Schleicher. He had made a deal with the Nazis, who had, that very same day, won the local majority. According to the deal, the ban on the SA would be removed and the Reichstag dissolved. Hindenburg, who approved the deal, would have his new cabinet handpicked by Schleicher. In turn, Hitler had to support the new government, something to which he readily agreed. Hitler and the Nazis could not be happier with the way things were turning out.

Chapter 15 – The Last Chancellor of the Republic

By 1933, economic depression still plagued the weary populace. Unemployment had reached a dizzying six million, and a third of the country's working population was jobless, restless, and angry.

After Brüning's humiliating tenure as chancellor, General Kurt von Schleicher became the real power behind the octogenarian president. He chose Hindenburg's new chancellor, the wealthy noble industrialist Franz von Papen, who had a dubious military record. Franz von Papen was a ridiculous figure of a man with a reputation as a crafty, vain, and ambitious intriguer. This blundering amateur politician had little experience on the national scene, as he had not even been a member of the Reichstag. Schleicher's own Centre Party immediately and unanimously ejected him from the party, indignant about his treachery toward Brüning.

Hitler, for his part, was biding his time until Schleicher upheld his part of the bargain. But that did not mean he was idle. In fact, he had not spent an idle moment since before the Beer Hall Putsch. All throughout the late 1920s and early 1930s, he and the Nazi Party were busy spreading their propaganda. These efforts, along with Hitler's magnetic and charismatic speeches, bolstered his public image. Hitler maligned the democratic system and communism, continually asserting that what Germany needed instead was a strong leader who would work in the interests of the nation and who could unite the country.

Although his Nazi Party did not specifically emphasize anti-Semitism during its propaganda campaign, it was certainly part of the agenda—and Hitler had an audience for it. He presented to the people a scapegoat for the Great Depression and the country's economic woes—the Jews. It reinforced rumors of the same nature that had been circulating for years.

In a time of crisis, Hitler offered the people stability. Germans were frightened and anxious about the country's future, so they clung to his words. Hitler seemingly wanted to give them the very thing they were desperately searching for. He played on the misery of the people, and while they languished, Hitler was pleased that he could use such poor conditions in his favor. Speaking about the deplorable state of the nation, he remarked, "Never in my life have I been so well disposed and inwardly contented as in these days. For hard reality has opened the eyes of millions of Germans."

His strategy to gain the trust and adoration of the people was working. The public flocked around him, and his popularity continued to attain new heights. And it was at that height that Hitler called for von Papen to make good on the pact that had been made with Schleicher. The new chancellor wasted no time. His first act was to dissolve the Reichstag and call for new elections at the end of July.

On June 16th, 1932, von Papen lifted the ban on the SA. It was like opening a cage containing frothing, ravenous wolves and letting them loose on an unsuspecting public. Almost immediately, shocking violence in the streets ensued, the likes of which the country had never seen before. Stormtroopers swarmed the streets, ready to fight and looking for blood, especially communist blood.

A virtual civil war erupted. During the first three weeks of June, Prussia alone saw an unbelievable 461 pitched battles in its streets, with 82 lives lost and over 400 injured. When the Nazis marched through Altona, a working-class suburb of Hamburg, 19 people ended up shot to death, and 285 were wounded in one day—and that was on top of the 18 killed the week before. The most shocking part? The Nazis had police escorts. It became obvious that the people could not look to that corner for protection.

Except for the Nazi and Communist Parties, all other political parties frantically called for von Papen to do something to halt the violence. The steps he took were mainly in his own interests and moved him one step closer to bringing down the last pillars of the republic and becoming the head of an authoritarian government. Martial law was declared, and von Papen deposed the Prussian government, boasting that "it only took a squad of soldiers to do it." More nails were being driven into the coffin of the crumbling republic.

Hitler and his men had similar goals to take down the republic, but von Papen would not be part of the plan. They would take him and his wealthy supporters down as well, calling von Papen's government a "transitional bourgeois cabinet." At this point, Hitler hardly even tried to conceal his intentions, brazenly telling von Papen that he considered his cabinet "only as a temporary solution" and that he would "continue to make his Nazi Party the strongest in the country." He then told von Papen point-blank, "The chancellorship will then devolve on me."

With the new Reichstag elections looming, Hitler and the Nazis threw themselves into furious campaigning, with Hitler giving speeches to the hundreds of thousands who turned out to hear him. They also reneged on their promise to support von Papen's government. Hitler no longer needed any of them, as his party was quickly gaining ground, bringing him closer and closer to his goal.

Hitler's campaigning had been effective. In the July elections, his party received more than 37 percent of the vote, making them the largest in the Reichstag. The Nazis felt victory within their grasp. Goebbels wrote, "Once we have the power we will never give it up. They will have to carry our dead bodies out of the ministries."

Hindenburg and von Papen began to panic, and in an effort to balance out the party's extremist tendencies, they proposed that Hitler's party join a coalition government. Hitler had the upper hand and was not interested unless they could sweeten the deal. He said the only way he would join a coalition was if he were made chancellor. Even Schleicher was becoming nervous and rolled back his position. Schleicher, now supporting von Papen's position, told Hitler he couldn't hope for anything more than a vice-chancellorship. Hitler was outraged at the suggestion and told them that it was all or nothing. The men, not wanting to make the decision, passed it on to von Hindenburg and declared that he would have the final word in the matter.

When the matter of the chancellorship did reach Hindenburg, he called Hitler into his office for discussions. Hitler went in, confident that he would get the chancellorship on his terms. But given the newness of the Nazi Party and the trouble they had stirred up, Hindenburg was not willing to concede. He stood firm that the chancellorship would only come with the agreement of a coalition government.

Hitler refused and left to brood. Though he squelched talks of another putsch, he was still gunning for von Papen, telling Nazi leader Hermann Rauschning, "we must be ruthless."

However confident he was, Hitler and his party's status was by no means set in stone. When the November Reichstag elections came around, his party's popularity slipped by two million votes. With the economy starting to recover, Hitler's promises of stability no longer seemed quite as necessary.

But in a fortunate turn of events, at least for Hitler, the Reichstag had lost confidence in von Papen. Setting his own sights on the chancellorship, Schleicher called for him to resign. Scrambling to keep power, von Papen tried to declare martial law, thereby setting himself up as a dictator. However, on December 2nd, General Eugen Ott came to von Papen with disturbing news. Government war game models showed that even under martial law, there would be no way to contain the Nazis and Communists. Deflated but not yet defeated, he realized that Schleicher was after his chancellorship and asked the president to fire him as defense minister. In a final indignity, von Hindenburg made Schleicher the chancellor instead.

Schleicher's star had risen, but it would quickly go into a meteoric fall, partly due to his own doing and partly with the help of a bitter and vengeful von Papen. The former chancellor was not ready to give up his position so easily, and he was determined to win it back. Still enjoying access to the president, he made every effort to disparage Schleicher.

The words von Papen spoke against the new chancellor stuck with the president and served to reinforce his own feelings about Schleicher. Though they had previously enjoyed a good rapport, the relationship was strained under the new arrangement. Used to von Papen's almost "servile devotion," Hindenburg was not endeared to Schleicher's brusque, self-centered manner.

Adding to it was von Hindenburg's own son, who, knowing both men, praised von Papen's "knightly fealty," a trait he felt Schleicher lacked.

Schleicher did not help his situation. When he took the chancellorship, von Hindenburg warned him not to speak out against his predecessor. Even though Schleicher agreed, it was obvious he was only telling the elderly president what he wanted to hear. Before long, Schleicher was speaking to journalists and publicly making sarcastic and cutting remarks about von Papen. Unbeknownst to him, some of those journalists had good relations with von Papen and turned around and told him the things Schleicher said. There is no doubt that von Papen reported these indiscretions to the president.

The divide between the two politicians further widened over Schleicher's failure to follow through on von Papen's agricultural policies, something else Schleicher had promised to do. But this time, Schleicher had a good reason. Realizing that Nazis had infiltrated the Agrarian League and were using it for their own agenda, he did not want to give in to their manipulations. The president, however, did not see what was happening, only the fact that these policies that were near to his heart were not being handled by Schleicher.

Meanwhile, von Papen conspired with Hitler behind Schleicher's back. Though Hitler had previously vowed to take von Papen down, the two men now needed each other. Nazi morale was low, conditions within the party were strained, and they were bankrupt. Their position seemed to be falling, so they had less leverage and bargaining power than the year before. Out of the chancellorship, von Papen was not faring much better. Von Papen suggested that they work to replace Schleicher with a Hitler-von Papen joint chancellorship. Hitler agreed to work it out.

Despite their efforts to keep the meeting secret, Hitler and von Papen did not know that Schleicher had tricks up his own sleeve. Von Papen must have been shocked when he saw their "secret" meeting blazing across newspaper headlines the next morning, with journalists blasting von Papen's disloyalty to Schleicher. Von Papen soon learned that Schleicher had spies of his own in the media. Schleicher's optimism soared, content that the revelation of von Papen's treachery would deal a death blow to any secret plans he had. Still, he continued to maneuver things to keep the Nazi threat contained.

By January 15th, 1933, Schleicher felt he had the situation well under control, so much so that he told the Austrian minister of justice that "Herr Hitler was no longer a problem, his movement had ceased to be a political danger, and the whole problem had been solved, it had been a thing of the past." But Schleicher was about to eat his words.

While Schleicher was boasting, the Nazis were handed a resounding win in the local elections in Lippe. The Nazis "beat the drum of victory," anticipating that things were again looking up for the party. But that "drumbeat" was also signaling the end for Schleicher.

Schleicher had failed to gain Nazi support or split up the party, and he did not have the support of the other major political parties. On January 23rd, he went to the president with a desperate plan. In an ironic twist, it was the same plan that von Papen had proposed just before his downfall, the same plan that Schleicher himself had rejected. He demanded that von Hindenburg employ Article 48 and use his emergency powers to dissolve the Reichstag. He then declared his intention to rule by decree, turning the government into a military dictatorship. Schleicher was now in the exact same spot for which he had condemned von Papen, but the only other option was to include Hitler in a presidential cabinet. It was very risky, and he was unwilling to take the chance of giving Hitler power.

But Hindenburg did not go for the plan any more than when it had been presented to him by von Papen. The president reiterated the same reasons for refusal that he had given the previous chancellor and told Schleicher to go find a Reichstag majority. But Schleicher had already failed in his efforts to do so. He knew he was finished. Everyone else knew it too. The next day, Goebbels reported, "Schleicher will fall any moment, he who brought down so many others." All of Schleicher's scheming and intrigue were seemingly coming back to him in a karmic twist.

Knowing it was the end for him, a disillusioned Schleicher visited the president on January 28th and tendered his resignation. Upon receiving the resignation, von Hindenburg told Schleicher, "I have already one foot in the grave and I am not sure that I shall not regret this action in heaven later on." Schleicher looked at the president and replied, "After this breach of trust, sir, I am not sure you will go to heaven." And with that, the last chancellor of the republic ended his brief fifty-seven days in office.

Chapter 16 – The End of the Republic and the Rise of the Third Reich

When von Papen heard of Schleicher's resignation, he did not waste a minute of time. By noon, he was in the president's office. Von Papen remembered his "secret" co-chancellorship conspiracy with Hitler, but for a moment, he flirted with the idea of double-crossing him and seizing the chancellorship for himself. But at the behest of the president, he instead agreed to find a way to form a government that included Hitler.

Hitler had not backed down in his demands for the chancellorship. So, von Papen believed that with Hitler actually taking part in the government, it would be easier to control him and the Nazis. He was also expecting to take over as commissar (governor) of Prussia, which he naively thought would allow him to keep the state's large police force from being used by the Nazis for their own nefarious purposes. His overconfidence in his ability to maintain control over Hitler and the Nazis was a fatal mistake. And the moves he would make over the next few days would be the catalyst for the disastrous events that followed.

Von Papen worked quickly to overcome any of Hindenburg's reservations about appointing Hitler as chancellor. He tried to convince Hindenburg that Hitler had taken a position of moderation and that Schleicher's conservative cabinet members were willing to work with him. He also remarked that a shake-up in the government, particularly the Defense Ministry, was needed, and Hindenburg agreed. By the end of the meeting, Hindenburg made von Papen promise that if Hitler were made chancellor, he would serve as vice-chancellor in order to keep the Nazis in check. It was not a firm commitment to the plan, but von Papen was happy to agree. Now, he would just have to get Hitler to agree to the terms.

Later that morning, he met with Hitler and gave him the terms. Von Papen sweetened the deal by not objecting to Hitler's cabinet appointments, and Hitler finally gave in to becoming chancellor with von Papen as the vice-chancellor. But Hitler had a new demand. Once he was chancellor, he wanted to immediately dissolve the Reichstag and call for a new election, with the intent of giving the Nazis greater representation in parliament. If all went according to plan, Hitler would be able to make laws and decrees without needing the consent of the Reichstag or even the president. He would use the republic's own democratic laws to his own advantage. Von Papen, eager to just get the ball rolling, did not object. He should have.

However, other prominent conservatives who were present vehemently objected. They saw Hitler as unscrupulous and fanatical, and they wanted nothing to do with helping him gain power. They instead proposed invoking emergency powers and creating an authoritarian government—one that did not include the Nazis.

Von Papen and German National People's Party leader Alfred Hugenberg were willing to take their chances with Hitler. They believed that they could use him for their own agenda, capitalizing on his popularity, and that the reward would be greater than the risk. But they would severely overestimate their ability to control Hitler once he had power. Hugenberg confidently told the objecting conservatives,

"We'll box Hitler in." Not convinced, they warned that Hitler was aiming to create a dictatorship. Von Papen dismissively replied, "You're mistaken. We've hired him!"

Schleicher, although having resigned, still threw in his two cents on the situation but only to advance his own career. At odds with von Papen, he knew he would not be able to keep control of the army as the minister of defense if von Papen took back the chancellorship. Because of that, he favored Hitler as chancellor, seeing it as the only way he could retain power. He, too, grossly overestimated his own value to Hitler and his regime. Seemingly unworried about what Hitler would do if he became chancellor, he even said that if Hitler created a dictatorship, he would simply make the army a "dictatorship within the dictatorship."

Misunderstandings, rumors, and paranoia soon caused chaos to break out. Hitler worried that a military coup was in the works, one that would interfere with his appointment to the chancellorship. He put the SA on alert to a possible putsch. Not long after, disturbing rumors reached the president.

The president was informed that Schleicher had mobilized the army and was planning a coup of his own. Allegedly, he was planning to depose Hindenburg and seize the presidency for himself. However, the rumor was completely unfounded. But Hindenburg and his family, who were inclined to believe that the defense minister was indeed unscrupulous enough to make such a move, took no pains to investigate the truth of it and denounced Schleicher as a traitor.

That moment of chaos worked in von Papen's favor. With the president somewhat distracted, he took the opportunity to catch Hindenburg off guard. Through several deceptions and ruses, which included false promises that Hitler's cabinet would not be dominated by Nazis, von Papen secured the agreement of the president to install a Hitler-led cabinet that night and appoint him to the chancellorship the next day.

Seeing that his only other option in this case was a military dictatorship, Hindenburg capitulated. The men promised each other that no meetings between Hitler and Hindenburg would take place without von Papen's presence, a tactic the president hoped would keep the radical Nazi leader in check.

The next day, Monday, January 30th, 1933, the president gave Hitler a short speech about political cooperation for the good of the nation. Hitler made promises he had no intention of keeping, and with that, he was sworn into office along with von Papen. Those loyal to the republic felt that the situation had just turned grave, but no one spoke out. Instead, they put all their hopes in Hindenburg being able to manage the situation.

The problem was, neither the elderly Hindenburg nor the conniving von Papen really knew Hitler and what he was capable of. They had not yet comprehended the strength of the forces he commanded nor the weaknesses of current institutions, like the army and churches, and other political parties in being able to stop him.

As Hitler stood at his office window after his swearing-in, thousands of stormtroopers triumphantly marched outside, parading and singing nationalistic songs. Hitler had pulled off a stunning political comeback given that during the election just thirty days earlier, his party was largely rejected by the public in a staggering setback.

But now, for the most part, Germans outside of the political arena were mostly indifferent to Hitler's appointment to the chancellorship. It hadn't even made headlines; instead, it was buried in the newspaper behind horse races and other sporting events. The people had seen so many governments and politicians come and go that this hardly made a difference to them. Many expected it to fail as the others had.

International observers, though, were more on edge. The Sunday Times of London asked if Hindenburg and von Papen "got Hitler into a cage before they wring his neck or are they in the cage?" A Swiss journalist bluntly pointed out that even with Hindenburg and von Papen there to ostensibly keep Hitler in check, "a bear is still a bear, even if you put a ring in its nose and lead it by a leash."

Though Hitler had been conferred great power, at the moment, he was sharing it with three other sources of authority. He had made promises of cooperating with them, knowing quite well that his first order of business would be to eliminate the power of the others and eventually find himself in full control.

Hardly twenty-four hours after Hitler came to office, he made his first move. Through manipulation and lies, Hitler's proposal for the dissolution of the Reichstag and new elections was accepted, albeit nervously and reluctantly. He assured von Papen and Hindenburg that no matter what the outcome of the election, the cabinet, which at the moment only contained three Nazi ministers, would remain unchanged.

With the new elections set, Hitler could use all the governmental resources available to win votes. With such resources as radio stations and the press at the Nazis' disposal, it would be easy to produce a huge propaganda campaign. The Nazis were jubilant, with Goebbels proclaiming, "Now it will be easy."

Next on Hitler's agenda was getting rid of the communist threat, and what happened next belied his flair for the dramatic and showed just what lengths the Nazis were willing to go to in order to achieve their ends.

On February 29th, as Hindenburg, von Papen, and Hitler were dining together, urgent news came that the Reichstag was on fire. At first, the men thought it to be a falsehood until they saw the red glow of flames through the window. The men raced to the Reichstag and were met by Göring, who immediately swore to heaven that it was "a Communist crime against the new government." Göring then went to the new Gestapo commander Rudolf Diels and proclaimed that there was a communist revolution in motion. He urgently yelled, "We must not wait a minute! We will show no mercy!" before ordering Diels to shoot every communist official and hang every communist deputy that very night. The plan was to conveniently eliminate any communists that could deny responsibility and do it quickly before an investigation could reveal the truth.

Of course, Hitler was going to exploit this event to the fullest, as it created the opportunity that he needed. The next day, he asked the president to sign a decree suspending seven articles of the constitution dealing with individual and civil liberties. He claimed it was for the "protection of the people and the state." The decree would also allow his government to take control of the federal states and make certain crimes punishable by death.

In one fell swoop, Hitler had given himself the power to legally outlaw his opposers and arrest them on trumped-up charges. The civil rights of average citizens were curtailed, and fear began to mount, as home searches and arrests could come at any time and for just about any reason. Freedom of speech became all but nonexistent.

The Communist Party was banned, and a spate of terrifying arrests followed. In less than one month, ten thousand communists, suspected communists, other well-known Germans, and a few Jews were arrested. Prisons and the SA barracks could not contain all the arrested, and the first concentration camps were opened. Those who were sent there were consigned to a life of ill-treatment, beatings, torture, and possibly even death.

When the time came for the March elections, the last democratic elections of the Weimar Republic and of Hitler's lifetime, Nazi supporters were the only campaigning voices that could be heard by the public. They instilled fear of a communist revolution and promised that only their party could bring about a "German paradise." In order to support this, more staged acts of terror followed the Reichstag fire. In a speech, Göring mockingly urged the communists to "struggle to the death" because he would be there to "grasp their necks and take them down."

Support for all other parties was all but silenced. Former Chancellor Brüning, however, refused to be quiet. He proclaimed that his Centre Party would resist the Nazis' rise and desperately pleaded with the president to "protect the oppressed against their oppressors." His appeal was met with silence from the president and the people.

When the time came for those early March elections, the Nazi Party managed to narrowly gain the Reichstag majority, thanks in part to the arrest of eighty-one Communist Party representatives. Hitler was one step closer to legally seizing absolute power. Now, he would have to get the majority of the Reichstag to agree to give it to him.

A few days later, Hitler made a "dazzling pledge" to the president and the people, capping it off with a display of false humility. In front of press cameras, he bowed low and took Hindenburg's hand in a Judas-like manner, knowing full well he was about to betray him. However, many were taken in by the display, with national and foreign political officials alike wondering how anyone could possibly deny Hitler full power after that rousing show of humility.

Just two days later, they received their answer. Hitler presented the Reichstag with the Enabling Act. In hindsight, the official title of the act, "Law for Removing the Distress of People and Reich," is almost laughable in its irony.

In the Enabling Act, Hitler requested full power to act without the consent of the vice-chancellor or president for four years. He stipulated that some of the laws he might pass "might deviate from the constitution" yet claimed that the powers of the president would remain "undisturbed." Hitler purposely presented himself as a modest and moderate man, duping the majority of the Reichstag. The German National Democrats, however, were not taken in by his show. They swore that no enabling act should give him the power he sought, as it would bring about the destruction of humanity, justice, freedom, and socialism.

Hitler, however, did not care in the least that he did not have their support. He dismissively told them, "You are no longer needed...Your death knell has sounded...I do not want your votes. Germany will be free but not through you!" Thunderous applause followed. It truly was a death knell, not just for the German National Democrats but also for the republic itself.

On March 23rd, the Enabling Act was passed. Hitler now had what he wanted—power without restraint and all national institutions under Nazi control. After Hitler came to power, Vorwärtseditor Friedrich Stampfer grimly spoke about the public nonchalance, saying, "Most people had no idea what had befallen them." What had befallen them was the sanctioned collapse of the republic and the beginning of the Third Reich's reign of terror.

Conclusion

After Hitler's victory, those who had helped him to power were then pushed into virtual irrelevance. Although Hindenburg and von Papen retained their positions for a time, they were essentially puppets, with Hitler pulling all the strings.

Alfred Hugenberg realized the gravity of what he had done. He said, "I yesterday committed the greatest stupidity of my life. I allied myself with the greatest demagogue in world history." His own ambitions thwarted and his alliance with Hitler souring after only five months, Hugenberg resigned and retired

Franz von Papen remained vice-chancellor, but his role in the government was gradually and purposefully marginalized by Hitler. Concerned about the loss of freedoms and terror the SA was spreading through the nation, von Papen gave the Marburg speech, condemning Hitler's actions. The speech incensed Hitler. Joseph Goebbels, then the propaganda minister, ordered that the speech not be played on the radio or written in the newspaper. But von Papen would not back down, telling Hitler unless he lifted the ban, he would resign and be happy to tell the president why. Hitler pretended to concede, but he was not through with von Papen.

Paul von Hindenburg remained president and was able to help restrain Hitler to some extent. By 1934, the elderly president was becoming alarmed by Hitler's excesses, particularly the violent activities propagated by the SA. He gave Hitler an ultimatum—rein in the SA or be removed from the chancellorship (after which the president would declare martial law and hand the government over to the military).

In a show of supposed loyalty to the president, Hitler soon instigated the Night of Long Knives, a night of extrajudicial executions of SA leaders, some of whom had been Hitler's confidants and allies. Among those who were executed was Ernst Röhm, the SA chief of staff and one of Hitler's long-time supporters. General Kurt von Schleicher also did not escape the purge; he and his wife were gunned down in their home.

During that night, the vice-chancellor's office was also ransacked, and von Papen was put under house arrest. His telephone line was cut, severing him from any outside communication and help. Once out of house arrest, an exhausted von Papen rushed to the chancellery only to find Hitler and the Nazis around a table with no place for him except a hole in the middle. He declared that his service to the Fatherland was over and resigned. However, Hitler would later appoint him as ambassador to Austria, a position in which he served until 1938.

When von Hindenburg finally died of lung cancer at eighty-six years of age, Hitler was already prepared to position himself as dictator. Hours before the failing president died, he had his cabinet pass a law stating that upon Hindenburg's death, the office of president would be abolished. Hitler would be the sole head of state. When Hindenburg died hours later, the last restraint around Hitler died with him.

The story of the Weimar Republic and its demise has become important to historians as a prime example of how democracy can fail. Many in Germany at first hailed it as the savior of the country.

Quickly enough, however, they began to despise it. Citizens conveniently blamed the abundant and severe problems the nation faced on the new democratic government instead of seeing that they were being divided by their own interests, leading to their failure to unite against Hitler and the Nazis.

However, the majority of the failure can be attributed to the ineptitude of those who were supposed to uphold democracy, as they were fighting and scheming among themselves instead of working for the good of the nation and effectively solving the severe issues from which the people were suffering. Professor of philosophy Igor Primoratz aptly called the republic a "democracy without democrats." And it ultimately led to Germany's downfall.

Here's another book by
Captivating History that you might like

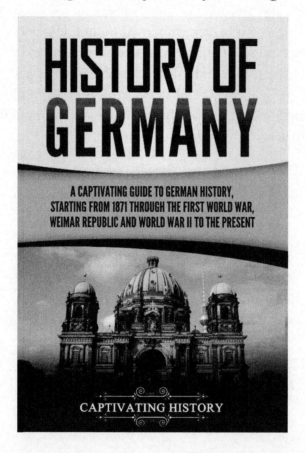

Free Bonus from Captivating History (Available for a Limited time)

Hi History Lovers!

Now you have a chance to join our exclusive history list so you can get your first history ebook for free as well as discounts and a potential to get more history books for free! Simply visit the link below to join.

Captivatinghistory.com/ebook

Also, make sure to follow us on Facebook, Twitter and Youtube by searching for Captivating History.

References

"Sailors' Revolt in Kiel." http://www.kurkuhl.de/en/novrev/films.html

"The Treaty of Versailles, 1919."
https://en.chateauversailles.fr/discover/history/key-dates/treaty-
versailles-1919

Goldberg, George (1965). The Peace to End Peace: The Paris Peace
Conference of 1919. New York, Harcourt, Brace & World.

Stone, Barry (2011). True Crime and Punishment: Mutinies,
Shocking Real-life Stories of Subversion at Sea. Sydney, N.S.W.:
Murdoch Books.

Horn, Daniel (1969). The German Naval Mutinies of World War I.
New Brunswick, New Jersey: Rutgers University Press.

"Encyclopedia - The Kiel Mutiny."
https://www.firstworldwar.com/atoz/kielmutiny.htm

"The Kiel fourteen points of the soldier's council."
https://germanhistorydocs.ghi-
dc.org/sub_document.cfm?document_id=3939 Translated from
German to English.

"Facing History & Ourselves; The Weimar Republic: The Fragility of
Democracy." https://www.facinghistory.org/weimar-republic-fragility-

democracy/politics/social-democratic-party-proclamation-republic-november-9-1918

Jones, Mark. "Kiel Mutiny. International Encyclopedia of the First World War." https://encyclopedia.1914-1918-online.net/article/kiel_mutiny

Britannica, The Editors of Encyclopedia. "Spartacus League." Encyclopedia Britannica, https://www.britannica.com/topic/Spartacus-League.

"Armistice on the Western Front." https://www.theworldwar.org/learn/armistice

Richard Cavendish. "The Spartacist Uprising in Berlin." Published in History Today. Volume 59 Issue 1 January 2009. https://www.historytoday.com/archive/spartacist-uprising-berlin

"Signing the Treaty of Versailles, 1919." EyeWitness to History. http://www.eyewitnesstohistory.com/ (2005).

Popa, Adriana (2010). "German citizens defend democracy against Kapp Putsch, 1920." https://nvdatabase.swarthmore.edu/content/german-citizens-defend-democracy-against-kapp-putsch-1920

"Kapp Putsch." https://schoolshistory.org.uk/topics/european-history/weimar-nazi-germany/kapp-putsch/

"The Weimar Republic." https://alphahistory.com/weimarrepublic/

King, Megan (2017). "Berlin's Most Illustrious Decade: A Brief History of Weimar Culture." https://theculturetrip.com/europe/germany/berlin/articles/berlins-most-illustrious-decade-a-brief-history-of-weimar-culture/

Goodman, George (pen name Adam Smith) (1981). Paper Money. G.K. Hall.

"Weimar Republic: Hyperinflation and the Invasion of the Ruhr." https://www.theholocaustexplained.org/the-nazi-rise-to-power/the-weimar-republic/invasion-of-the-ruhr/

"Weimar Hyperinflation."
http://www.johndclare.net/Weimar_hyperinflation.htm

Lowe, Norman (1982). Mastering Modern World History.

"A Hoax of Hate: The Protocols of the Learned Elders of Zion."
https://www.adl.org/resources/backgrounders/a-hoax-of-hate-the-protocols-of-the-learned-elders-of-zion

"Gustav Stresemann – Biographical." NobelPrize.org. Nobel Prize Outreach AB 2021.
https://www.nobelprize.org/prizes/peace/1926/stresemann/biographical/

United States Holocaust Memorial Museum. German Rentenmark.
https://collections.ushmm.org/search/catalog/irn524926

Kyle Roderick. "In Hyperinflation's Aftermath, How Germany Went Back to Gold." https://www.forbes.com/2011/06/09/germany-gold-standard.html?sh=56a98f9a5934

Gordon, Harold J., Jr. Hitler and the Beer Hall Putsch. Princeton, N.J.: Princeton University Press, 1972.

Shirer, Lawrence. The Rise and Fall of the Third Reich: A History of Nazi Germany, Volume 2. Simon & Schuster.

Peukert, Detlev (1992). The Weimar Republic: The Crisis of Classical Modernity. New York: Hill and Wang.

C N Trueman. "The Young Plan of 1929."

historylearningsite.co.uk. The History Learning Site, 22 May 2015.

The Great Depression
https://encyclopedia.ushmm.org/content/en/article/the-great-depression

"End of the Weimar Republic."
https://www.bbc.co.uk/bitesize/guides/zp34srd/revision/1

"The End of the Weimar Republic." John Wheeler-Bennett. Foreign Affairs.

Vol. 50, No. 2 (Jan., 1972), pp. 351-371 (21 pages) Published By: Council on Foreign Relations

https://www.jstor.org/stable/20037911

Turner, Henry Ashby (1996). Hitler's Thirty Days to Power: January 1933. Reading, Massachusetts: Addison-Wesley.

Printed in Great Britain
by Amazon

40423777R10069